The Federal TSP Cookbook:
Investment Recipes for the Thrift Savings Plan

By

R. Ron Elmer, MBA, CFA, CPA, CFP®

**If you can bake brownies,
you can manage your investments!**

Also by R. Ron Elmer

The 401k Cookbook

The Rollover IRA Cookbook

The ETF Cookbook

Disclaimer: There are no warranties, expressed or implied, as to the accuracy, completeness, or results obtained from any information in this book. Past performance does not guarantee future results.

Warning: Past performance does not guarantee future results. Investment returns and principal value will fluctuate, so that investors' shares, when sold, may be worth more or less than their original cost. Investing in any mutual fund, passively or actively managed, does not guarantee that an investor will make money, avoid losing capital, or indicate that the investment is risk-free. Actively managed funds sometimes outperform passive index funds. We just don't know in advance which actively managed funds will outperform the relevant index. An index mutual fund does not guarantee performance superior to an actively managed mutual fund. There are no absolute guarantees in investing.

Ron is not a federal employee and invests many of his own personal assets via ETFs at TD Ameritrade and in Vanguard Mutual Funds that are similar to the TSP Funds.

www.InvestorCookbooks.com

This one is for Keith, Pat, Trek, Trey, Walt and
all the other federal employees that make our country great!

Table of Contents

Part 1

How to Use This Book

How to Use This Book

Use this book like you would use any cookbook full of recipes.
But, first, you need to determine which recipe might work best for you by following these simple steps:

Step #1

Take the quiz.
Begin by taking the short, 12-question quiz designed to gauge your risk tolerance. Do you like your investments *spicy* or *mild*?

Step #2

Find your recipe.
Take the total points from your quiz score and adjust your age. After determining your "risk-adjusted investment age," go find the recipe number that is closest to it.

Step #3

Call ThriftLine at (877) 968-3778 or (404) 233-4400.
Or, go to **www.tsp.gov** and request to invest your Thrift Savings Plan account to match your recipe.

Step #4 (Optional)

Read the rest of the book.
"Investing Basics" and "Investing Details" explain investments and outline my opinions and rationales for my suggested recipes. Discover the answer to the question "How Much is Enough?" in the last two sections.

Part 2

The Quiz

Let's Get Cooking:
What Is Your Appetite for Risk?

In 5 minutes we'll find out if you like your investments *mild* or *spicy!* (There are no right or wrong answers here. The point values are neither good nor bad.)

(1) If your entire investment portfolio were to fall by 35 percent in one year (perhaps 2008), are you most likely to be:

+3 horrified?
+1 concerned?
 0 hungry, so you bake some brownies?
-3 excited by the opportunity to invest at lower prices?

(2) If a single investment within your account were to fall by 50 percent in just one year (perhaps 2008), are you most likely to:

+3 sell all of it?
+1 sell some of it?
 0 eat a whole plate of brownies?
-3 buy more?

(3) I am willing to accept higher short-term volatility (ups and downs) in my investments in order to achieve higher long-term returns.

+3 Strongly disagree.
+1 Somewhat disagree.
-1 Somewhat agree.
-3 Strongly agree.

(4) I am willing to accept lower returns in order to avoid short-term volatility (ups and downs) in my investments.

-3 Strongly disagree.
-1 Somewhat disagree.
+1 Somewhat agree.
+3 Strongly agree.

(5) I check the value of my investments:

    0 every quarter.
  +1 never, because I am afraid to look.
  +2 every month.
  +3 every day.
  +4 several times per day.

(6) I know the difference between a stock and a bond and an ETF.

  -3 Yes.
   0 No, but I am going to read the last chapter of this book.
  +3 No, and I don't really want to know

(7) I plan to begin withdrawing money from my investment portfolio when I am:

  +3 sixty years old.
   0 sixty-five years old.
  -3 seventy years old.

(8) Do you have any health issues that could possibly prevent you from working until your projected retirement age?

  +5 Yes.
   0 No.
  +2 Possibly.

(9) In addition to my personal retirement savings (401(k) and IRAs), I am expecting to receive monthly payments from a pension fund when I retire.

  -3 Yes.
   0 No.

(10) My current annual income is:

      0   less than $100,000 per year.
    -1   more than $100,000 per year.
    -3   more than $200,000 per year.

(11) My current income varies significantly from` year to year.

   +3   Yes.
    0   No.

(12) All of my investments and savings combined (IRA + 401(k) + 403(b) + TSP) total:

     0   less than $1 million.
    -2   more than $1 million.
    -4   more than $2 million.

Total from all answers above: _____

Enter your age: _____

Add the above two numbers =   _____

This is your risk-adjusted investment age.

Now go find the recipe in the next section of this book that corresponds to your number.

Part 3

Investment Recipes

Under 20 Year Old
Federal Thrift Savings Plan Recipe

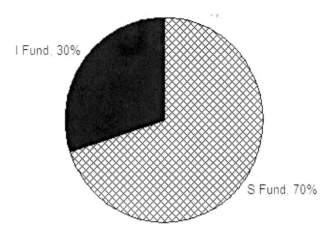

I Fund, 30%

S Fund, 70%

Allocation*	TSP Fund Name	TSP Symbol
30%	International Stock Index	I Fund
70%	Small Capitalization Stock Index	S Fund

100%

Approximate Annual Portfolio Expenses = 0.03%

What the Under-20 recipe could make BEFORE expenses:	
Long-term Annual Return Guesstimate	10.4%
Average Annual Return (past 15 years)	7.6%
Actual 15-Year Cummulative Return	201.9%
Current Yield	1.0%

Will this recipe upset your stomach?	Best	Worst
Best / Worst 1-year return (past 15 years)	67.5%	-46.9%
Best / Worst 3-year period return (past 15 years)	29.9%	-18.9%
Annualized Standard Deviation (a risk measure)		18.7%
Number of years this recipe lost money (in last 15)		4

* Rebalance your portfolio on your birthday *each* year for five years, then move to the next recipe in this book.

20-24 Year Old
Federal Thrift Savings Plan Recipe

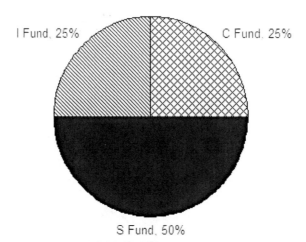

Allocation*	TSP Fund Name	TSP Symbol
25%	International Stock Index	I Fund
50%	Small Capitalization Stock Index	S Fund
25%	Common Stock Index	C Fund
100%		

Approximate Annual Portfolio Expenses = 0.03%

What the 20-year old recipe could make BEFORE expenses:	
Long-term Annual Return Guesstimate	10.1%
Average Annual Return (past 15 years)	7.5%
Actual 15-Year Cummulative Return	194.5%
Current Yield	1.2%

Will this recipe upset your stomach?	Best	Worst
Best / Worst 1-year return (past 15 years)	63.8%	-46.1%
Best / Worst 3-year period return (past 15 years)	26.8%	-17.8%
Annualized Standard Deviation (a risk measure)		17.8%
Number of years this recipe lost money (in last 15)		4

* Rebalance your portfolio on your birthday *each* year for five years, then move to the next recipe in this book.

25-29 Year Old
Federal Thrift Savings Plan Recipe

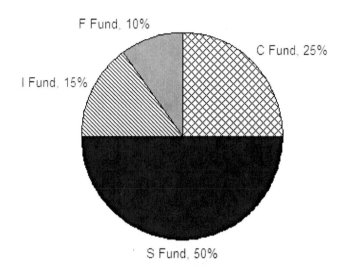

F Fund, 10%

C Fund, 25%

I Fund, 15%

S Fund, 50%

Allocation*	TSP Fund Name	TSP Symbol
15%	International Stock Index	I Fund
50%	Small Capitalization Stock Index	S Fund
25%	Common Stock Index	C Fund
10%	Fixed Income Index	F Fund
100%		

Approximate Annual Portfolio Expenses = 0.03%

What the 25-year old recipe could make BEFORE expenses:	
Long-term Annual Return Guesstimate	9.5%
Average Annual Return (past 15 years)	7.7%
Actual 15-Year Cummulative Return	206.0%
Current Yield	1.3%

Will this recipe upset your stomach?	Best	Worst
Best / Worst 1-year return (past 15 years)	55.5%	-40.6%
Best / Worst 3-year period return (past 15 years)	24.4%	-15.1%
Annualized Standard Deviation (a risk measure)	15.7%	
Number of years this recipe lost money (in last 15)	4	

* Rebalance your portfolio on your birthday *each* year for five years, then move to the next recipe in this book.

30-34 Year Old
Federal Thrift Savings Plan Recipe

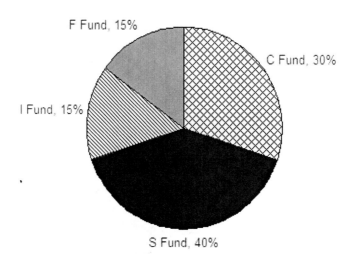

Allocation*	TSP Fund Name	TSP Symbol
15%	International Stock Index	I Fund
40%	Small Capitalization Stock Index	S Fund
30%	Common Stock Index	C Fund
15%	Fixed Income Index	F Fund
100%		

Approximate Annual Portfolio Expenses = 0.03%

What the 30-year old recipe could make BEFORE expenses:	
Long-term Annual Return Guesstimate	9.2%
Average Annual Return (past 15 years)	7.7%
Actual 15-Year Cummulative Return	202.1%
Current Yield	1.5%

Will this recipe upset your stomach?	Best	Worst
Best / Worst 1-year return (past 15 years)	50.8%	-38.1%
Best / Worst 3-year period return (past 15 years)	23.3%	-13.6%
Annualized Standard Deviation (a risk measure)		14.4%
Number of years this recipe lost money (in last 15)		4

* Rebalance your portfolio on your birthday *each* year for five years, then move to the next recipe in this book.

35-39 Year Old
Federal Thrift Savings Plan Recipe

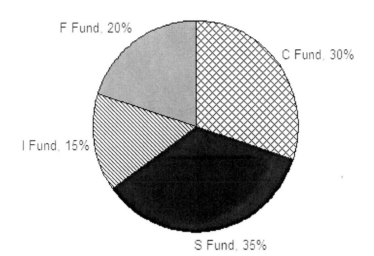

Allocation*	TSP Fund Name	TSP Symbol
15%	International Stock Index	I Fund
35%	Small Capitalization Stock Index	S Fund
30%	Common Stock Index	C Fund
20%	Fixed Income Index	F Fund
100%		

Approximate Annual Portfolio Expenses = 0.03%

What the 35-year old recipe could make BEFORE expenses:	
Long-term Annual Return Guesstimate	8.9%
Average Annual Return (past 15 years)	7.6%
Actual 15-Year Cummulative Return	200.7%
Current Yield	1.6%

Will this recipe upset your stomach?	Best	Worst
Best / Worst 1-year return (past 15 years)	47.1%	-35.7%
Best / Worst 3-year period return (past 15 years)	22.1%	-12.3%
Annualized Standard Deviation (a risk measure)		13.4%
Number of years this recipe lost money (in last 15)		4

* Rebalance your portfolio on your birthday *each* year for five years, then move to the next recipe in this book.

40-44 Year Old
Federal Thrift Savings Plan Recipe

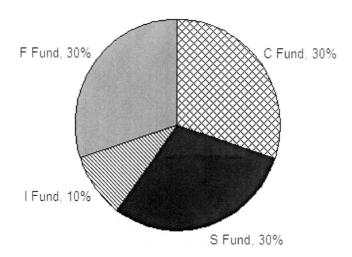

Allocation*	TSP Fund Name	TSP Symbol
10%	International Stock Index	I Fund
30%	Small Capitalization Stock Index	S Fund
30%	Common Stock Index	C Fund
30%	Fixed Income Index	F Fund
100%		

Approximate Annual Portfolio Expenses = 0.03%

What the 40-year old recipe could make BEFORE expenses:	
Long-term Annual Return Guesstimate	8.2%
Average Annual Return (past 15 years)	7.6%
Actual 15-Year Cummulative Return	201.2%
Current Yield	1.9%

Will this recipe upset your stomach?	Best	Worst
Best / Worst 1-year return (past 15 years)	40.5%	-30.6%
Best / Worst 3-year period return (past 15 years)	20.6%	-9.6%
Annualized Standard Deviation (a risk measure)		11.5%
Number of years this recipe lost money (in last 15)		4

* Rebalance your portfolio on your birthday *each* year for five years, then move to the next recipe in this book.

45-49 Year Old
Federal Thrift Savings Plan Recipe

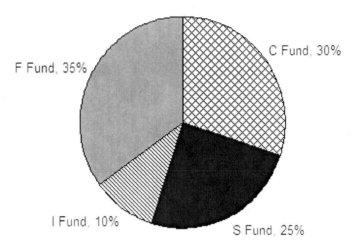

Allocation*	TSP Fund Name	TSP Symbol
10%	International Stock Index	I Fund
25%	Small Capitalization Stock Index	S Fund
30%	Common Stock Index	C Fund
35%	Fixed Income Index	F Fund
100%		

Approximate Annual Portfolio Expenses = 0.03%

What the 45-year old recipe could make BEFORE expenses:	
Long-term Annual Return Guesstimate	7.9%
Average Annual Return (past 15 years)	7.6%
Actual 15-Year Cummulative Return	197.8%
Current Yield	2.0%

Will this recipe upset your stomach?	Best	Worst
Best / Worst 1-year return (past 15 years)	37.4%	-28.2%
Best / Worst 3-year period return (past 15 years)	19.5%	-8.3%
Annualized Standard Deviation (a risk measure)		10.5%
Number of years this recipe lost money (in last 15)		4

* Rebalance your portfolio on your birthday *each* year for five years, then move to the next recipe in this book.

50-54 Year Old
Federal Thrift Savings Plan Recipe

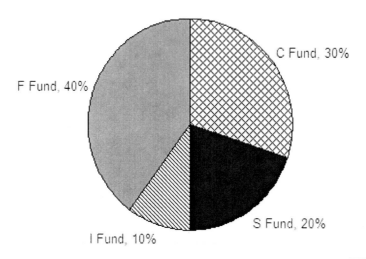

Allocation*	TSP Fund Name	TSP Symbol
10%	International Stock Index	I Fund
20%	Small Capitalization Stock Index	S Fund
30%	Common Stock Index	C Fund
40%	Fixed Income Index	F Fund
100%		

Approximate Annual Portfolio Expenses = 0.03%

What the 50-year old recipe could make BEFORE expenses:	
Long-term Annual Return Guesstimate	7.6%
Average Annual Return (past 15 years)	7.5%
Actual 15-Year Cummulative Return	193.8%
Current Yield	2.1%

Will this recipe upset your stomach?	Best	Worst
Best / Worst 1-year return (past 15 years)	34.4%	-25.8%
Best / Worst 3-year period return (past 15 years)	18.4%	-6.9%
Annualized Standard Deviation (a risk measure)		9.6%
Number of years this recipe lost money (in last 15)		4

* Rebalance your portfolio on your birthday *each* year for five years, then move to the next recipe in this book.

55-59 Year Old
Federal Thrift Savings Plan Recipe

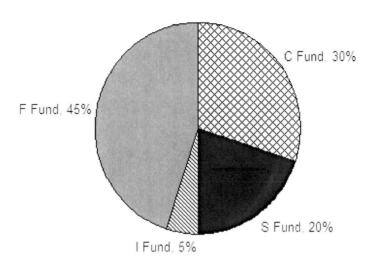

Allocation*	TSP Fund Name	TSP Symbol
5%	International Stock Index	I Fund
20%	Small Capitalization Stock Index	S Fund
30%	Common Stock Index	C Fund
45%	Fixed Income Index	F Fund
100%		

Approximate Annual Portfolio Expenses = 0.03%

What the 55-year old recipe could make BEFORE expenses:	
Long-term Annual Return Guesstimate	7.4%
Average Annual Return (past 15 years)	7.5%
Actual 15-Year Cummulative Return	194.5%
Current Yield	2.2%

Will this recipe upset your stomach?	Best	Worst
Best / Worst 1-year return (past 15 years)	31.8%	-23.2%
Best / Worst 3-year period return (past 15 years)	18.0%	-5.5%
Annualized Standard Deviation (a risk measure)		8.7%
Number of years this recipe lost money (in last 15)		4

* Rebalance your portfolio on your birthday *each* year for five years, then move to the next recipe in this book.

60-64 Year Old
Federal Thrift Savings Plan Recipe

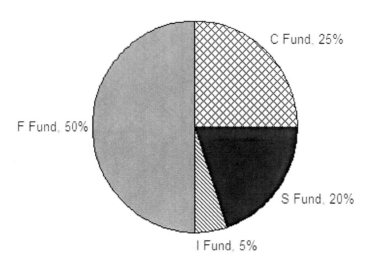

Allocation*	TSP Fund Name	TSP Symbol
5%	International Stock Index	I Fund
20%	Small Capitalization Stock Index	S Fund
25%	Common Stock Index	C Fund
50%	Fixed Income Index	F Fund
100%		

Approximate Annual Portfolio Expenses = 0.03%

What the 60-year old recipe could make BEFORE expenses:	
Long-term Annual Return Guesstimate	7.0%
Average Annual Return (past 15 years)	7.4%
Actual 15-Year Cummulative Return	193.3%
Current Yield	2.3%

Will this recipe upset your stomach?	Best	Worst
Best / Worst 1-year return (past 15 years)	29.6%	-20.9%
Best / Worst 3-year period return (past 15 years)	16.9%	-4.3%
Annualized Standard Deviation (a risk measure)		8.0%
Number of years this recipe lost money (in last 15)		4

* Rebalance your portfolio on your birthday *each* year for five years, then move to the next recipe in this book.

65-69 Year Old
Federal Thrift Savings Plan Recipe

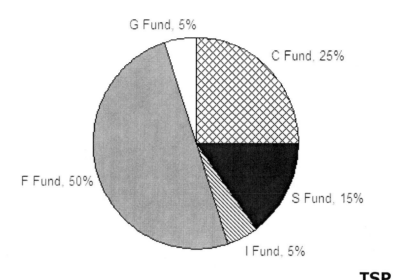

Allocation*	TSP Fund Name	TSP Symbol
5%	International Stock Index	I Fund
15%	Small Capitalization Stock Index	S Fund
25%	Common Stock Index	C Fund
50%	Fixed Income Index	F Fund
5%	Government Securities	G Fund
100%		

Approximate Annual Portfolio Expenses = 0.03%

What the 65-year old recipe could make BEFORE expenses:	
Long-term Annual Return Guesstimate	6.6%
Average Annual Return (past 15 years)	7.3%
Actual 15-Year Cummulative Return	187.7%
Current Yield	2.4%

Will this recipe upset your stomach?	Best	Worst
Best / Worst 1-year return (past 15 years)	26.9%	-18.6%
Best / Worst 3-year period return (past 15 years)	15.8%	-3.1%
Annualized Standard Deviation (a risk measure)		7.2%
Number of years this recipe lost money (in last 15)		3

* Rebalance your portfolio on your birthday *each* year for five years, then move to the next recipe in this book.

Acknowledgments

I would like to thank Dr. Richard Warr, Associate Professor of Finance at North Carolina State University's College of Management, for his help and input as a sounding board for this project. Special thanks to my former boss, Carl Davis, for his help and encouragement. Thanks also goes out to my family—including my sister Cheryl Elmer; my parent-in-laws Tom and Janet Cassady; my brother-in-law Kevin Cassady; and especially my wife Cori—who read drafts and provided valuable input that resulted in needed changes to this book. And to my friends, Paige Henderson, Pat Vesper, Michael Hollenbach, and Gene Farelly, who also contributed good ideas resulting in a better book, thank you.

70-74 Year Old
Federal Thrift Savings Plan Recipe

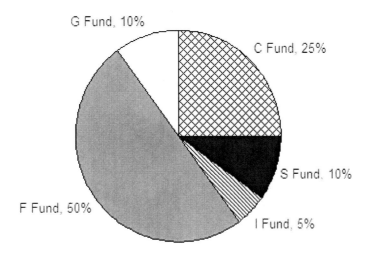

Allocation*	TSP Fund Name	TSP Symbol
5%	International Stock Index	I Fund
10%	Small Capitalization Stock Index	S Fund
25%	Common Stock Index	C Fund
50%	Fixed Income Index	F Fund
10%	Government Securities	G Fund
100%		

Approximate Annual Portfolio Expenses = 0.03%

What the 70-year old recipe could make BEFORE expenses:	
Long-term Annual Return Guesstimate	6.2%
Average Annual Return (past 15 years)	7.1%
Actual 15-Year Cummulative Return	181.6%
Current Yield	2.5%

Will this recipe upset your stomach?	Best	Worst
Best / Worst 1-year return (past 15 years)	24.4%	-16.2%
Best / Worst 3-year period return (past 15 years)	14.6%	-2.1%
Annualized Standard Deviation (a risk measure)		6.4%
Number of years this recipe lost money (in last 15)		2

* Rebalance your portfolio on your birthday *each* year for five years, then move to the next recipe in this book.

75-79 Year Old
Federal Thrift Savings Plan Recipe

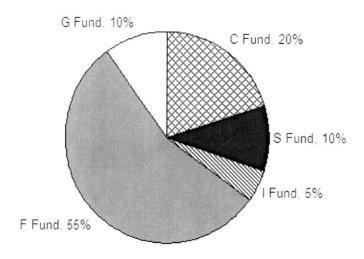

G Fund, 10%
C Fund, 20%
S Fund, 10%
I Fund, 5%
F Fund, 55%

Allocation*	TSP Fund Name	TSP Symbol
5%	International Stock Index	I Fund
10%	Small Capitalization Stock Index	S Fund
20%	Common Stock Index	C Fund
55%	Fixed Income Index	F Fund
10%	Government Securities	G Fund
100%		

Approximate Annual Portfolio Expenses = 0.03%

What the 75-year old recipe could make BEFORE expenses:	
Long-term Annual Return Guesstimate	6.0%
Average Annual Return (past 15 years)	7.1%
Actual 15-Year Cummulative Return	179.0%
Current Yield	2.6%

Will this recipe upset your stomach?	Best	Worst
Best / Worst 1-year return (past 15 years)	22.5%	-14.3%
Best / Worst 3-year period return (past 15 years)	13.6%	-1.1%
Annualized Standard Deviation (a risk measure)		5.8%
Number of years this recipe lost money (in last 15)		2

* Rebalance your portfolio on your birthday *each* year for five years, then move to the next recipe in this book.

80-84 Year Old
Federal Thrift Savings Plan Recipe

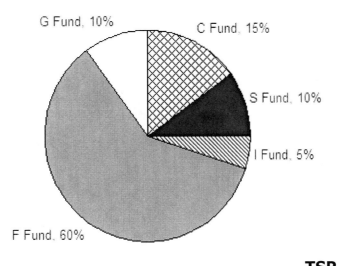

Allocation*	TSP Fund Name	TSP Symbol
5%	International Stock Index	I Fund
10%	Small Capitalization Stock Index	S Fund
15%	Common Stock Index	C Fund
60%	Fixed Income Index	F Fund
10%	Government Securities	G Fund
100%		

Approximate Annual Portfolio Expenses = 0.03%

What the 80-year old recipe could make BEFORE expenses:	
Long-term Annual Return Guesstimate	5.7%
Average Annual Return (past 15 years)	7.0%
Actual 15-Year Cummulative Return	176.1%
Current Yield	2.7%

Will this recipe upset your stomach?	Best	Worst
Best / Worst 1-year return (past 15 years)	20.8%	-12.5%
Best / Worst 3-year period return (past 15 years)	12.6%	-0.2%
Annualized Standard Deviation (a risk measure)		5.2%
Number of years this recipe lost money (in last 15)		2

*** Rebalance your portfolio on your birthday *each* year for five years,
then move to the next recipe in this book.**

85-89 Year Old
Federal Thrift Savings Plan Recipe

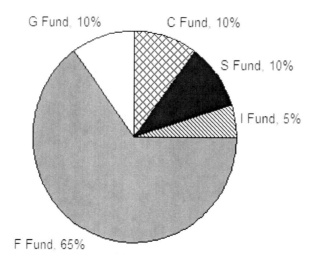

Allocation*	TSP Fund Name	TSP Symbol
5%	International Stock Index	I Fund
10%	Small Capitalization Stock Index	S Fund
10%	Common Stock Index	C Fund
65%	Fixed Income Index	F Fund
10%	Government Securities	G Fund
100%		

Approximate Annual Portfolio Expenses = 0.03%

What the 85-year old recipe could make BEFORE expenses:	
Long-term Annual Return Guesstimate	5.5%
Average Annual Return (past 15 years)	6.9%
Actual 15-Year Cummulative Return	172.8%
Current Yield	2.8%

Will this recipe upset your stomach?	Best	Worst
Best / Worst 1-year return (past 15 years)	19.0%	-10.6%
Best / Worst 3-year period return (past 15 years)	11.5%	0.7%
Annualized Standard Deviation (a risk measure)		4.7%
Number of years this recipe lost money (in last 15)		1

* Rebalance your portfolio on your birthday *each* year for five years, then move to the next recipe in this book.

90-94 Year Old
Federal Thrift Savings Plan Recipe

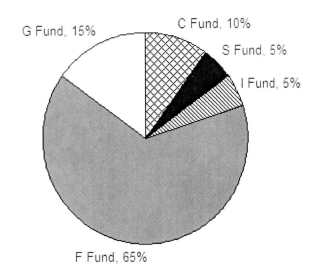

Allocation*	TSP Fund Name	TSP Symbol
5%	International Stock Index	I Fund
5%	Small Capitalization Stock Index	S Fund
10%	Common Stock Index	C Fund
65%	Fixed Income Index	F Fund
15%	Government Securities	G Fund
100%		

Approximate Annual Portfolio Expenses = 0.03%

What the 90-year old recipe could make BEFORE expenses:	
Long-term Annual Return Guesstimate	5.1%
Average Annual Return (past 15 years)	6.8%
Actual 15-Year Cummulative Return	169.2%
Current Yield	2.9%

Will this recipe upset your stomach?	Best	Worst
Best / Worst 1-year return (past 15 years)	17.2%	-8.7%
Best / Worst 3-year period return (past 15 years)	10.5%	1.6%
Annualized Standard Deviation (a risk measure)		4.3%
Number of years this recipe lost money (in last 15)		1

* Rebalance your portfolio on your birthday *each* year for five years, then move to the next recipe in this book.

95-99 Year Old
Federal Thrift Savings Plan Recipe

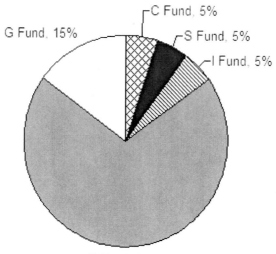

C Fund, 5%

G Fund, 15%

S Fund, 5%

I Fund, 5%

F Fund, 70%

Allocation*	TSP Fund Name	TSP Symbol
5%	International Stock Index	I Fund
5%	Small Capitalization Stock Index	S Fund
5%	Common Stock Index	C Fund
70%	Fixed Income Index	F Fund
15%	Government Securities	G Fund
100%		

Approximate Annual Portfolio Expenses = 0.03%

What the 95-year old recipe could make BEFORE expenses:	
Long-term Annual Return Guesstimate	4.8%
Average Annual Return (past 15 years)	6.6%
Actual 15-Year Cummulative Return	161.2%
Current Yield	3.0%

Will this recipe upset your stomach?	Best	Worst
Best / Worst 1-year return (past 15 years)	15.5%	-6.6%
Best / Worst 3-year period return (past 15 years)	9.5%	2.5%
Annualized Standard Deviation (a risk measure)		3.9%
Number of years this recipe lost money (in last 15)		1

* Rebalance your portfolio on your birthday *each* year for five years, then move to the next recipe in this book.

100+ Year Old
Federal Thrift Savings Plan Recipe

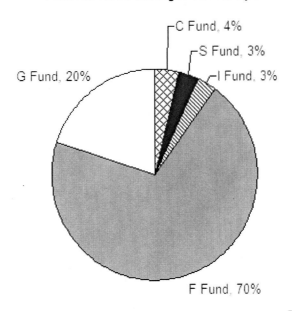

Allocation*	TSP Fund Name	TSP Symbol
3%	International Stock Index	I Fund
3%	Small Capitalization Stock Index	S Fund
4%	Common Stock Index	C Fund
70%	Fixed Income Index	F Fund
20%	Government Securities	G Fund
100%		

Approximate Annual Portfolio Expenses = 0.03%

What the 100-year old recipe could make BEFORE expenses:	
Long-term Annual Return Guesstimate	4.4%
Average Annual Return (past 15 years)	6.5%
Actual 15-Year Cummulative Return	156.5%
Current Yield	3.1%

Will this recipe upset your stomach?	Best	Worst
Best / Worst 1-year return (past 15 years)	14.8%	-4.3%
Best / Worst 3-year period return (past 15 years)	9.0%	2.9%
Annualized Standard Deviation (a risk measure)		3.7%
Number of years this recipe lost money (in last 15)		none

* Rebalance your portfolio on your birthday *each* year for five years, then move to the next recipe in this book.

Part 4

Investing Basics

Essentials for the Investment Chef

1. If you can bake brownies, you can manage your own investments.
2. Stocks beat bonds over the long term.
3. Everyone is a long-term investor.
4. Bonds are less risky than stocks in the short run.
5. Stocks are less risky than bonds over the long run (due to inflation risk).
6. The allocation between stocks and bonds is your most important decision.
7. You only own bond funds (F Fund) in order to smooth the ride and keep you from panicking and selling everything when stock funds perform poorly.
8. When stocks fall in value, usually bonds rise (but not the "G Fund" in the Thrift Savings Plan).
9. Your stock funds *will* perform poorly at some point while you own them.
10. Corporate bonds tend to lose value when stocks lose value.
11. Treasury Inflation Protected Securities (TIPS) are the only bonds guaranteed to beat inflation *and* severe deflation (Unfortunately, these are currently not an option within the Thrift Savings Plan).
12. Small company stocks (S Fund) will beat large company stocks (C Fund) over the long run.
13. Small company stock funds *will* be more volatile than large company stock funds in the short run.
14. Don't buy individual stocks or bonds.
15. Buy mutual funds or ETFs (Exchange-Traded Funds).
16. Don't pay commissions to buy mutual funds or ETFs (buy "no load" funds or commission-free ETFs).

17. Given a choice, buy funds with the lowest expense ratios.

18. Buy index funds wherever possible.

19. Sprinkle in some actively managed funds in small company stocks and foreign stocks *only* if you plan to research the fund managers closely.

20. It is rare for a fund to beat a passive index over the long run.

21. Index funds will beat the vast majority of other funds in the long run.

22. There will always be a few funds that beat their benchmark index.

23. If each of 1,000 monkeys managed stock funds and picked the stocks by throwing darts at *The Wall Street Journal,* half of them would beat the Standard and Poor's 500 Index (S&P 500).

24. Less than half of all mutual funds beat the S&P 500.

25. It is easy to find funds that beat their benchmark index in the *past*.

26. It is *very* difficult to pick funds that will beat their index benchmark in the *future*.

27. Don't invest in Real Estate Investment Trust (REIT) funds.

28. Don't invest in commodities.

29. Stay away from "alternative" investments in general.

30. If you see the term "fund of funds," think "fees on fees."

31. Don't try to "time" the market (don't try to buy stock funds when you think the stock market is going up or selling when you think it will go down).

32. Even the pros can't time the market consistently.

33. You might guess correctly and sell stock funds before they fall further, but you will also likely fail to buy back that fund before it rises significantly.

34. A few investment "gurus" will successfully call the next market top (or bottom).

35. Those same "gurus" will call 7 of the next 2 market tops (or bottoms).

36. Consistently invest more money each month (unless you are not working).

37. Do NOT "buy and hold." Instead, "buy and rebalance." Rebalance your portfolio *once, each* and *every* year (to help you remember, do it on your birthday).

38. Own foreign stock funds (I Fund) for diversification, but don't over do it.

39. Foreign stocks tend to go down when U.S. stocks also go down.

40. Either value or growth investment styles will outperform for short periods.

41. Over the long run, value and growth will be a tie.

42. If you own both growth and value funds, you have created an expensive core portfolio.

43. Simplify and just buy core or blend funds (index where possible).

44. All TSP funds are index funds – that's a good thing.

45. If you have significant investments outside your retirement plan, own index stock funds outside the retirement plans and bond funds inside the tax-sheltered retirement plans.

46. Don't give your money to anyone who will earn a commission on the sale.

47. Don't borrow from your 401(k) or TSP plan.

48. *Never* buy your company's stock within your 401(k) plan unless you *have* to. (Use the G Fund sparingly within the TSP).

49. Don't withdraw money from your TSP or 401(k) or IRA before you are 59 1/2 years old.

50. If you have a 401(k) plan, save $16,500 each year ($22,000 if you are over 50).

51. Your long-term goal is to save 22 times your annual expenses in order to retire.

52. Withdraw only 4.5 percent from your savings annually to avoid outliving your money.

53. Don't ruin brownies by not following the recipe exactly.

54. Don't make stuff up just to make your list end in a round number.

Part 5

Investing Details

Introduction

If you can bake brownies, you can manage your investments. You don't even need to read this final chapter if you've already taken the brief quiz from earlier in this book and found a recipe you liked.

Okay, if you are reading this sentence, then you are most likely the inquisitive type that might want to know why you should add half a teaspoon of salt and baking powder to your brownie batter. Most folks just put the half teaspoon of salt and baking powder into the bowl because Betty Crocker or Paula Deen said so. Ah, but you are not one of them. You wonder how these foul-tasting ingredients could possibly make chocolate and butter taste any better than they already do. Plus, Dr. Oz was on *Oprah,* and he told you that salt is bad for your blood pressure. You figure, "hey, maybe I won't even notice the missing salt" and thereby add years to your life by eating salt-free brownies. But, alas, you soon find out that there is a method to the madness of the basic brownie recipe.

Brownies just are not the same without the missing ingredient. The same can be true for the investment recipes in this book. Honestly, I am neither Emeril Lagasse nor even Guy Fieri and therefore cannot answer the question as to why half a teaspoon of salt and baking powder would make brownies taste better. And while I am also not Warren Buffett or Peter Lynch, I can let you in on the secrets that drive the recipes in this book so you can avoid a flat, shrunken retirement account.

Here is a quick primer on investments with secrets that no one will tell you, since many investment pros don't know some of this (or don't want you to know).

What's the difference between a stock and a bond?

You can separate investments between stocks and bonds.

Bonds

Bonds (also called fixed income investments) are the equivalent to lending money to a company or the government. By buying a bond, you lend them $1,000, and they might pay 6 percent interest for 5 years and then give you back the original $1,000. If this were a company, you would have lent them money, and they would have run their business as they'd see fit. Bondholders have no say in how the company is run and will not earn a share of the profits. However, if the company declares bankruptcy, the bondholders get paid their money first, before anything is given to stock investors.

Corporate bonds are considered a little more risky than government bonds since a corporation can go bankrupt. If the U.S. government goes bankrupt, we'll have bigger problems than worrying about our investments. Thus, corporate bonds generally pay a higher interest rate than government bonds. However, corporate bond performance return is more correlated to the stock market than U.S. government bonds and, therefore, do not provide as much diversification to a portfolio when the economy goes into a recession.

Over the last 70 years or so, bonds have returned a fairly steady average of 5–6 percent in value. Bond investments fall when interest rates rise. It is rare for bonds to lose more than 5–10 percent in a single year, but they do lose value occasionally. Likewise, it is rare for bonds to return more than 10–15 percent in value in a single year, but it has happened. So you can think of bonds as being less risky than stocks (until I let you in on a secret).

Stocks

When you buy a company's stock, you are now an owner of a portion of the company and can share in the profits (or losses) and have a say in how the company is run. For example, say you own just one share of Microsoft. Each year the company will vote on certain things, and by owning that one share in the company, you get one vote on the issue at hand. However, if the company goes bankrupt, the bondholders will get some (probably not all) of their money back, and you would probably get zero.

When buying a stock, you actually own part of the company, and when buying a bond, you are actually lending the company money. When I taught college courses in finance, I would use the following example to further define the difference between a stock and a bond.

When most people buy a house they usually put down 20 percent of their own money, but borrow 80 percent of the purchase price from a bank. In this situation, you actually own the house even though the bank put up more of the money than you did. Even though the bank has more money at risk than you, the bank cannot tell you what color to paint your house. The bank lent you the money, but you own the house. Of course, if you stop making payments to the bank, they become owners of the house (and may decide to paint the house a different color). The same is true in the bond market. If a company stops making interest payments on their bonds, then the bond holders will become the owners of the company, and the stockholders will be left with nothing.

Within stocks, you can further break things down into stocks of foreign companies (international stocks) and domestic stocks (U.S.-based companies). We can also break down domestic stocks into large companies (large caps), medium-sized companies (mid caps), and small companies (small caps). Generally, small caps are more risky than large caps, but they offer a greater return.

Over the last 70 years or so, stocks have returned an average of 10–12 percent, but they have also been known to lose or gain 50 percent in a single year. So stocks are more risky than bonds.

I believe the lower end of the long-term historical returns for stocks are achievable for the future. In addition, I believe long-term future returns will continue to outpace returns on bonds. The stocks in the Dow Jones Industrial Average currently trade at a price/earnings (P/E) ratio of around 15. If you flip this multiple upside down, you get an earnings yield of nearly 7 percent. Currently, 30-year bonds yield just 4 percent. Even if earnings for companies do not grow, the earning yields of stocks are higher than the yield on bonds. If earnings in corporate America just keep pace with inflation of, say, 3 percent (or more), you can see long-term returns of 10 percent are achievable in the stock market.

Here is where the first secret comes in: while bonds are less risky over a short period of time (say, 5 years), bonds are actually more risky over a long period of time. Why? Let's first talk about inflation risk.

Inflation Risk

Here is an example. Let's say you buy a supposedly low-risk bond issued by Johnson & Johnson. You give them $1,000 and they agree to pay 6 percent interest for the next 10 years. Inflation right now is only 3 percent, so you would have a real return of 3 percent (6% − 3% = 3%). Did you know that in the 1970s we saw inflation that was greater than 10 percent? What if high inflation comes back during your 10-year holding period of that bond? At the end of the 10 years, you may not have lost money on paper, but in its real purchasing power, you will actually be poorer.

So if high inflation comes back, would you rather own a Johnson & Johnson bond? Or would you rather own the company that makes the drugs that are increasingly more expensive? Inflation is a rise in prices of goods (such as drugs). If drugs get more expensive by 10 percent each year, it might be good to own the company that is charging the ever-increasing prices (and earning the ever-increasing profits).

So bonds, or bank CDs, or anything that pays a known interest rate is less risky but only over shorter periods of time. For longer time horizons, your biggest risk is inflation risk, and stocks are actually less risky!

TIPS

In the past few years the U.S. government has invented a new type of bond. They are called Treasury Inflation Protected Securities (TIPS). These bonds pay a fixed rate of interest, but the value of the bond is pegged to inflation. With a typical bond, you might pay $1,000 for it and receive 6 percent interest for 5 years. After 5 years, you would be repaid the $1,000. With TIPS, your $1,000 face value of the bond would grow with inflation. So if inflation totaled 10 percent over the 5-year period in the example above, you would be repaid with $1,100 at the end of 5 years instead of just $1,000 with the typical bond. In effect, TIPS will give you a guaranteed return over inflation of approximately 1–3 percent.

What's even better, TIPS protect you against deflation (when prices of goods go down). Deflation was a major problem during The Great Depression in the 1930s. If deflation rears its ugly head again, TIPS will protect you on the downside as the principle value of a TIPS bond will not go below the original $1,000 face value. So TIPS protect you from both inflation and deflation. I wish the Thrift Savings Plan had a TIPS fund, but it does not.

Examples (Ticker Symbol):
Vanguard Inflation-Protected Securities Fund (VIPSX)
iShares Barclays TIPS Bond Fund ETF (TIP)

Mutual Funds

Mutual funds represent a collection of people who pool their money, with the mutual fund manager deciding which stocks or bonds (or both) to buy (this is what I used to do for a living). This is how most people should invest since they don't have enough money to get the appropriate amount of diversification (i.e., don't have enough money to spread across 100 different stocks). Funds are more efficient, less expensive, and you don't have to research hundreds of companies. The mutual fund manager does this for you.

When investing in mutual funds, you want to buy no-load funds, preferably without redemption fees. Loads are up-front fees paid immediately upon your first purchase, and they are ridiculous to pay. Why pay 2–8 percent up front for the privilege of investing in a fund when you don't have to? Many funds have redemption fees, which act as incentives for you not to sell. Don't invest in funds with high redemption fees that require you to invest for many years. It may be reasonable to invest in a no-load fund with a 1 percent redemption fee to be paid if you sell within one year. But it does not make sense to pay a 7 percent load up front and another redemption fee of 7 percent when you sell the fund 6 years later.

We are about to get to another secret! There are two ways to invest in mutual funds in all the asset categories you have to choose from: (1) index funds and (2) actively managed funds.

Most mutual funds are actively managed. This means the fund's manager buys and sells investments in an effort to "beat the index." Index funds don't try to beat the index and instead just passively buy and hold all stocks (or bonds) in the index. All Thrift Savings Plan funds are passive index funds – and that is a good thing.

Exchange-Traded Funds (ETF)

Exchange-Traded Funds or ETFs are index funds that trade like a stock. This provides one benefit over a traditional "mutual fund." A mutual fund can only be purchased at the close of the trading session each day – usually 4:00 PM Eastern Time. Even if you place an order to purchase a mutual fund at 10:00 AM, your order will not be priced and processed until 4:00 PM.

With an ETF, if you purchase at 10:00 AM you get the price of the ETF at 10:00 AM and do not have to wait until 4:00 PM. Thus, if you are in a hurry to get into the market, the ETF is your best option.

However, one downside to purchasing an ETF can be the fact that you may have to pay a commission or transaction fee to purchase. Since an ETF trades like a stock, you must purchase it like a stock and that typically entails paying a commission. However, TD Ameritrade has made more than 100 ETFs "commission-free." Every recipe in "The ETF Cookbook" uses only ETFs that are available commission-free at TD Ameritrade. An investor could easily use these recipes at any brokerage, but at the time of this writing, only TD Ameritrade offered commission-free ETF trades for all of the ETFs used in this book.

Most ETFs are passively managed index funds and have very low expenses embedded in the funds – much lower than a typical traditional mutual fund. I highly recommend index investing for the vast majority of individual investors.

So what's an index? The most famous index is the Dow Jones Industrial Average, but it is not really that important since it only includes 30 stocks. Another index you may have heard of is the S&P 500 Index. Indexes are a collection of stocks (or bonds) that have been added up to give people an idea of how those investments have performed on average.

Following are some examples of important indexes.

Large Company Stocks (C Fund)

Long-term return expectation equals 9–10 percent or 5–6 percent over inflation.

The Standard and Poor's 500 Index (S&P 500) is the most common large cap index. It is a collection of 500 large company stock prices (most companies in the index have a market value or capitalization of over $5 billion).

Using this index, you can measure the performance of large cap mutual funds. Here is the second secret: in any given year roughly 50 percent of large cap mutual funds do *not* "beat" the S&P 500 Index. Over longer periods of time, I would expect fewer than 20 percent to beat the S&P 500. *Kiplinger's Magazine* found that just 31 percent of large company mutual funds beat the S&P 500 Index over the 15-year period ending June 30, 2009.

Once you take taxes into consideration, even fewer active mutual funds beat the index because you will have to pay capital gains taxes each time the fund sells a stock. Index funds, on the other hand, rarely sell stocks and therefore, rarely pass through capital gains to be taxed to their investors. However, keep in mind that taxes are not important within your 401(k) or traditional IRA where your gains are not taxable until you take money out. And, with a Roth IRA, your gains will never be taxed.

The truth is that there is so much publicly available information on large companies that it is difficult to gain an advantage over the millions of other investors that have access to the same information. If a company has problems, everyone knows it, and it is reflected in a lower stock price. So by the time a fund manager figures it out, the stock price has already fallen before he or she can sell it. If there is good news, everyone hears it at the same time, and the stock price will already have risen before a fund manager can buy it. It is even more difficult now that we have the Internet. It is a very efficient market and results in a loser's game that can't be won (without one being lucky).

So some funds beat the index, but it is highly unlikely that you or I would be smart enough (or lucky enough) to pick one that will beat the index consistently, especially once taxes are considered. Index funds have lower expense ratios than actively managed funds. You have maybe a 1-in-10 chance of picking a fund that will beat the S&P 500 index fund over 10 years. The average large cap fund will lose to the index by 2 percent per year. A typical mutual fund has a 1 percent annual expense ratio that often could be as high as 2 percent. These expenses make it even harder for actively managed funds to beat index funds with very low expenses. In short, the lower the expense ratio, the better. My recommendation is to invest in an index fund for large cap stock investing.

Examples (Ticker Symbol):
Vanguard 500 Index Fund (VFINX)
iShares S&P 500 Index Fund ETF (IVV)

Expenses Matter

You may think 1 or 2 percent is not much to worry about. But, 1 or 2 percent per year for 30 years turns out to be a huge difference.

Annual Return	Annual Investment	Value in 30 years
7%	$3,000	$283,382
9%	$3,000	$408,923

In the table above you can see that an increase in return of 2 percent per year on an annual investment of $3,000 per year over 30 years would translate into an increase of $125,541 or 44 percent! (125,541 / 283,382)

Overall, Vanguard has the lowest average expense ratios across its mutual funds at just 0.23 percent, compared to 1.19 percent average across all mutual funds, according to Morningstar. An investor can save approximately $960 per year on an investment of $100,000 using Vanguard funds versus the typical fund family. With expenses of less than 0.03 percent, the TSP expenses are likely the lowest among any savings plan anywhere in the world!

Mid-sized Company Stocks (S Fund)

Long-term return expectation is equal to 10–11 percent or 6–7 percent over inflation.

The S&P 400 Mid Cap Index and the Russell Mid Cap Index are the most common mid cap indexes. The S&P 400 is a collection of 400 mid-sized companies (with market values of between $1.5 and $5.0 billion). Most mid cap managers use the Russell Mid Cap Index as their benchmark. It is a significantly bigger benchmark than the S&P 400 Index. For example, the largest company in the S&P 400 Index rarely cracks the top 50 in the Russell Mid Cap Index.

Because it is more difficult to gain information on mid-sized companies than large companies, mid cap mutual fund managers actually have a better chance of beating this index. Compared to large cap managers, a mid cap manager should have a little better odds to beat the mid cap index before taxes are considered. However, *Kiplinger's Magazine* found just 12 percent of mid cap mutual funds beat the S&P 400 Mid Cap Index over the past 15 years, and just 27 percent won over the last 5 years.

My recommendation: within a tax-sheltered investment like a 401(k) or IRA, go ahead and pair an active manager with a good low-cost index fund if you don't mind doing the research required to pick a good one. Otherwise, make your life simple, and use an index fund here as well (with preference to an index fund tracking the S&P 400 Mid Cap Index). Outside a tax-sheltered vehicle, absolutely use the more tax efficient index fund.

The Small Capitalization Stock Index Fund (S Fund) is actually an index fund that includes both mid-cap and small-cap stocks.

Examples (Ticker Symbol):
Vanguard Mid-Cap Index Fund (VIMSX)
Vanguard Mid-Cap ETF (VO)

Small Company Stocks (S Fund)

Long-term return expectation is equal to 11–12 percent or 7–8 percent over inflation.

The Russell 2000 Index is the most common small cap index. It's a collection of 2000 smaller companies (market values of these companies are typically below $2 billion). The S&P Small Cap 600 is another less popular index.

The small cap market is less efficient than the large cap market, which makes the odds of a good manager beating the index much better. *Kiplinger's Magazine* found that 53 percent of small cap managers beat the S&P Small Cap 600 Index over the 15-year period ending June 30, 2009, but just 36 percent outperformed over the past 5 years. I suspect the S&P 600 is tougher to beat than the Russell 2000 Index. I'd guess roughly 70–80 percent of small cap managers will beat the Russell 2000 Index going forward.

Generally, my recommendation is to index at least half of your allocation in the small cap market (preferably an index fund that tracks the S&P Small Cap 600 Index and *not* the Russell 2000), and put the other half with an active manager with a good track record of consistently beating this index.

Examples (Ticker Symbol):
Vanguard Small-Cap Index Fund (NAESX)
Vanguard Small-Cap ETF (VB)

Picking Actively Managed Funds

Make sure that the manager who beat the index is still managing the fund and has not left. The historical performance of a fund, as reported by the fund, does not change just because the manager has left. Thus, if there is a new manager, the historical performance of the fund is meaningless, and you should not rely on it. Buying a mutual fund after a key manager has left would be the equivalent of betting on the Cleveland Cavaliers to win the NBA championship, not knowing that LeBron James had left the team to join the Miami Heat.

If your favorite mutual fund company does not have a good active small cap fund, or if you don't want to do the homework and keep up with an actively managed fund, just go ahead and buy a good index fund.

This brings us to another important point. When picking an actively managed fund, it is best to find a fund that is managed as a team. If the team loses one person, it is not a big deal. Also, the fund should be large enough that you know it will be around for a long time, but not too large so that it is difficult for the managers to manage. This is very important for small cap investing. In my opinion, funds under $100 million are too small, and funds over $2 billion are too big.

International Stocks (I Fund)

Long-term return expectation is equal to 10–11 percent, or 6–7 percent over inflation.

The MSCI EAFE index is the most common international stock index. It includes stocks of companies in Europe, Australia, and the Far East.

The international stock market is also inefficient, and international stock funds have historically beaten this index, but it seems to be getting tougher over time. *Kiplinger's Magazine* found that 56 percent of international mutual funds beat the MSCI EAFE Index over the past 15 years, but just 47 percent did so the past 5 years ending June 30, 2009. Still, I would recommend using a good active manager for this asset class if possible and pairing it with a low-cost international index fund. If you don't want the hassle of keeping tabs on an active manager, just buy a good low-cost index fund.

Examples (Ticker Symbol):
Vanguard Total International Stock Index Fund (VGTSX)
Vanguard MSCI EAFE ETF (VEA)

Bonds (F Fund)

Long-term return expectation is equal to 5–6 percent, or 1–2 percent over inflation.

Bond managers have several indexes, with Barclays Aggregate Bond Index (formerly known as the Lehman Aggregate) being the most popular. Like stock fund managers, most bond fund managers have a difficult time beating their index (especially after taxes, if not held within a tax-sheltered 401(k) or IRA). So, once again, I would recommend the use of low-expense index funds.

Bonds can be segregated in several ways, but the most useful distinction is made by length of maturity. Short-term bonds (G Fund) are the least volatile and typically have a maturity of two years or less. Long-term bonds have the highest price volatility and are typically defined as maturities of ten years or longer. Intermediate-term bonds (F Fund) are usually defined as between two years and ten years in maturity.

ETF Examples (Ticker Symbol):
Vanguard Short-Term Bond ETF (BSV)
Vanguard Intermediate-Term Bond ETF (BIV)
Vanguard Long-Term Bond ETF (BLV)

Vanguard Mutual Fund Examples (Ticker Symbol):
Vanguard Short-Term Bond Index Fund (VBISX)
Vanguard Intermediate-Term Bond Index Fund (VBIIX)
Vanguard Long-Term Bond Index Fund (VBLTX)

Asset Allocation

So here are your typical choices within an IRA or 401(k) plan:

1. Bonds—short-term fixed income (G Fund)
2. Bonds—intermediate-term fixed income (F Fund)
3. Bonds—long-term fixed income (F Fund)
4. Bonds—inflation protected (TIPS are not in TSP)
5. Stocks—large cap (C Fund)
6. Stocks—mid cap (S Fund)
7. Stocks—small cap (S Fund)
8. Stocks—foreign (I Fund)

Okay. Now that you know the best way to invest in each area, you are wondering how much to put in each asset class. If you have not already done so, go to the beginning of this book and take the quiz. Then, go find your appropriate investment recipe.

The first thing to understand is why you need these 8 different asset classes. The reason is for diversification. You want a little of all eight due to their respective correlations of returns with each other to smoothen the performance. Sometimes when stocks perform poorly, bonds do very well. Take the year 2000, when bonds returned a surprising 12 percent, while large cap stocks fell 9 percent. The year before, large cap stocks were up 21 percent, while bonds were down 2 percent. The trick would be to be in stocks in 1999 and then switch to bonds in 2000. The problem is that no one has been able to consistently predict when you should be in one and not the other. You might get lucky a couple of years in a row, but over a long period of time, studies have shown that you do more harm than good trying to get in and out at the right time (again, especially when taxes are a consideration).

Some Like It Hot, but (Older) Gentlemen Prefer Bonds

Since stocks have had a long-term return higher than bonds, you want as much stock as possible and still be able to sleep at night when the stock market goes through a down period. Here is my suggestion.

Take a few minutes and **study the chart on the next page**.

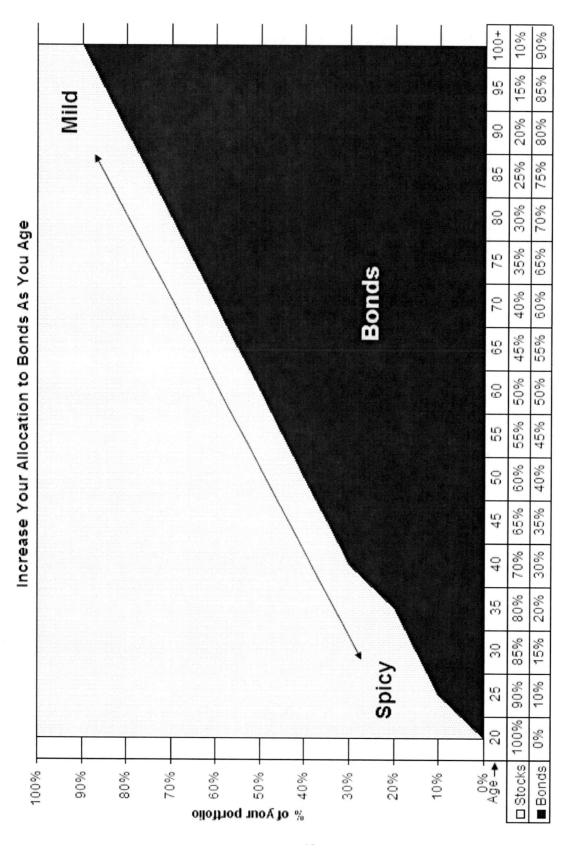

Increase Your Allocation to Bonds As You Age

Age	20	25	30	35	40	45	50	55	60	65	70	75	80	85	90	95	100+
☐ Stocks	100%	90%	85%	80%	70%	65%	60%	55%	50%	45%	40%	35%	30%	25%	20%	15%	10%
■ Bonds	0%	10%	15%	20%	30%	35%	40%	45%	50%	55%	60%	65%	70%	75%	80%	85%	90%

48

Until you are 25 years old, allocate 100 percent of your investments toward stock mutual funds. At 25, begin adding to a Treasury Inflation Protected Securities (TIPS) mutual fund. Do not begin buying a traditional fixed income bond fund until you are 35 years old (perhaps younger or older, depending on how you scored on your risk tolerance quiz at the beginning of this book).

As you age, you should move roughly 1 percent per year from stocks and into bonds. So when you are 60 years old and probably near retirement, you will have 50 percent bonds and 50 percent stocks. When you are 80 and statistically near death, you will be 30/70 stocks/bonds, which is good; just in case you live to be 100, the stocks will ensure you don't "outlive" your money. Many older people are too conservative and can't stomach having any money in the stock market. These people will be in big trouble if they live to be 100, and high inflation comes back (which it probably will at some point over a 100-year period).

When I worked for a pension fund, I spent a lot of time doing statistical correlation analysis of the different asset classes. Again, the only reason to invest in all asset classes is that they move up and down at different times, and this smoothes performance of your total portfolio, allowing you to sleep at night instead of worrying about your investments. I found that there was no reason to have more than 10–20 percent of your total stock portfolio in international stocks.

Within the domestic stock market, large companies make up roughly 85 percent of the stock market, 7 percent are mid-sized companies, and 8 percent are small companies. Remember that smaller stocks have tended to outperform larger stocks over long periods of time, but their returns are also more volatile.

Take a few minutes and **study the chart on the next page**.

Best and Worst Annual Returns for Last 10 Years
For Each Recipe by Age

100% Stocks

50% Stocks
50% Bonds

10% Stocks
90% Bonds

Age

■ Best 12 months   □ Worst 12 months

You will notice that as you add bonds to your portfolio as you age, the maximum return for your portfolio goes down, but the volatility of returns also goes down. When you are younger, you have more time to recover from a downturn in the stock market. So my portfolio recipes are spicier for the young, with more stocks, but they get less spicy as people age, with more bonds.

Rebalance Your Portfolio Annually

Each year some asset classes will do better than others. Thus, your portfolio will get "*out of balance*" over time if you don't keep an eye on it. Every time the tires on your car get out of balance, you end up with a bumpy ride. The same can happen with your investment portfolio. My suggestion is for you to rebalance your portfolio annually on your birthday. Look at your investment recipe and make sure your portfolio is exactly where it should be once each and every year. This works pretty well over time as you "*buy low*" and "*sell high*" year after year.

Do not try to dart in and out between stock funds and bond funds in an attempt to "*time the market.*" That is a loser's game as everyone tends to zig when the stock market zags. You, and everyone else, will surely get it wrong time and time again. This will cost you plenty over the long haul. But, also do NOT be a "*buy and hold*" investor. Instead, think "*buy and rebalance, buy and rebalance, buy and rebalance,*" year, after year, after year.

Take a few minutes, and **study the chart on the next page**.

The Reason Why You Need Diversification

(and the reason why you need to rebalance your portfolio EVERY year)

21 Years of Annual Returns by Asset Class

Best → Worst

2001	2002	2003	2004	2005	2006	2007	2008	2009	2010	21-Year Average Return	Risk
Interm. Bonds 9%	TIPS Bonds 17%	Small Stocks 46%	Foreign Stocks 21%	Foreign Stocks 16%	Foreign Stocks 27%	Foreign Stocks 16%	Long Bonds 8%	MidCap Stocks 40%	Small Stocks 28%	MidCap Stocks 14%	MidCap Stocks 19%
Long Bonds 9%	Long Bonds 15%	Foreign Stocks 40%	MidCap Stocks 21%	MidCap Stocks 14%	Small Stocks 16%	TIPS Bonds 12%	Interm. Bonds 5%	Foreign Stocks 40%	MidCap Stocks 26%	Small Stocks 11%	Small Stocks 19%
Short Bonds 8%	Interm. Bonds 13%	MidCap Stocks 34%	Small Stocks 20%	Small Stocks 8%	Large Stocks 16%	Interm. Bonds 7%	Short Bonds 5%	Small Stocks 36%	Large Stocks 15%	Large Stocks 11%	Large Stocks 19%
TIPS Bonds 8%	Short Bonds 8%	Large Stocks 29%	Large Stocks 11%	Large Stocks 5%	MidCap Stocks 14%	Short Bonds 7%	TIPS Bonds -2%	Large Stocks 26%	Foreign Stocks 11%	Foreign Stocks 8%	Foreign Stocks 22%
Small Stocks 7%	MidCap Stocks -15%	TIPS Bonds 8%	Long Bonds 9%	Long Bonds 5%	Short Bonds 4%	Long Bonds 7%	Small Stocks -36%	TIPS Bonds 11%	Long Bonds 10%	TIPS* Bonds 7%	TIPS* Bonds 6%
MidCap Stocks -1%	Foreign Stocks -15%	Interm. Bonds 6%	TIPS Bonds 8%	TIPS Bonds 3%	Interm. Bonds 4%	MidCap Stocks 6%	Large Stocks -37%	Interm. Bonds 7%	Interm. Bonds 9%	Long Bonds 7%	Long Bonds 4%
Large Stocks -12%	Small Stocks -20%	Long Bonds 6%	Interm. Bonds 3%	Interm. Bonds 2%	Long Bonds 3%	Large Stocks 5%	MidCap Stocks -42%	Short Bonds 5%	TIPS Bonds 6%	Interm. Bonds 7%	Interm. Bonds 5%
Foreign Stocks -21%	Large Stocks -22%	Short Bonds 3%	Short Bonds 2%	Short Bonds 1%	TIPS Bonds 0%	Small Stocks 1%	Foreign Stocks -46%	Long Bonds 2%	Short Bonds 4%	Short Bonds 6%	Short Bonds 3%

52

The Reason Why You Need Diversification

(and the reason why you need to rebalance your portfolio EVERY year)

21 Years of Annual Returns by Asset Class

Best → Worst	1990	1991	1992	1993	1994	1995	1996	1997	1998	1999	2000
Best	Short Bonds 10%	MidCap Stocks 50%	Small Stocks 18%	Foreign Stocks 33%	Foreign Stocks 8%	Large Stocks 38%	Large Stocks 23%	Large Stocks 33%	Large Stocks 29%	Foreign Stocks 27%	MidCap Stocks 18%
	Long Bonds 10%	Small Stocks 46%	MidCap Stocks 12%	Small Stocks 19%	Large Stocks 1%	MidCap Stocks 31%	MidCap Stocks 19%	MidCap Stocks 32%	Foreign Stocks 20%	Small Stocks 21%	Long Bonds 10%
	Interm. Bonds 9%	Large Stocks 31%	Large Stocks 8%	MidCap Stocks 14%	Short Bonds 1%	Small Stocks 28%	Small Stocks 17%	Small Stocks 22%	MidCap Stocks 19%	Large Stocks 21%	Interm. Bonds 10%
	Large Stocks -3%	Interm. Bonds 15%	Interm. Bonds 7%	Large Stocks 10%	Long Bonds -2%	Interm. Bonds 15%	Foreign Stocks 6%	Interm. Bonds 8%	Long Bonds 8%	MidCap Stocks 15%	Short Bonds 8%
	MidCap Stocks -5%	Long Bonds 14%	Long Bonds 7%	Interm. Bonds 9%	Small Stocks -2%	Long Bonds 14%	Short Bonds 5%	Long Bonds 8%	Interm. Bonds 8%	Short Bonds 3%	Small Stocks -3%
	Small Stocks -20%	Foreign Stocks 12%	Short Bonds 6%	Long Bonds 8%	Interm. Bonds -2%	Foreign Stocks 11%	Long Bonds 4%	Short Bonds 7%	Short Bonds 7%	Long Bonds 0%	Large Stocks -9%
Worst	Foreign Stocks -23%	Short Bonds 12%	Foreign Stocks -12%	Short Bonds 5%	MidCap Stocks -4%	Short Bonds 11%	Interm. Bonds 4%	Foreign Stocks 2%	Small Stocks -3%	Interm. Bonds 0%	Foreign Stocks -14%

53

I'd like to point out a few things about the diversification chart above:

In the last 21 years, EVERY asset class has been the BEST and the WORST performer at least once (and no one knows which will be best at any time).

Look at how often the BEST performer in one or more years becomes the WORST performer very soon and vice versa (this is why you must rebalance your portfolio each year). Take Foreign Stocks as an example: They were bottom performers from 1990-92, the best 1993-94, worst in 1997 to best in 1998-99 and back to worst in 2000-2001. Foreign stocks then had an incredible run from 2003-2007 only to be punished in 2008 and nearly cut in half!

A stock class has been first in 17 out of 21 years while bonds have been first just 4 out of 21. (This is why you need stock mutual funds even if you are 80 years old.)

Interm. Bonds = Intermediate Bonds

TIPS = Treasury Inflation Protected Securities (these are a relatively new type of bond I consider a separate, and very important asset class beginning in 2001). TIPS long-term return and risk data are based on 10 years.

Risk = Standard Deviation (a measure of variability in annual returns).

That chart makes a great case for why you need diversification and why you need to rebalance your portfolio each and every year.

For example, if large cap stocks have a really good year (like they did in 1999), you will be "overweight" in large cap stocks at the end of the year. So you would sell some large cap stocks, and move the money into the asset class in which you were "underweight" due to their relatively poorer performance. For example, you might have sold large cap stocks and bought bonds after their poor performance in 1999. That would have worked out pretty well since stocks did poorly in 2000, and bonds did very well (exactly the opposite of what they did in 1999).

Rebalancing is pretty easy to do within a tax shelter like 401(k), 403(b), or IRA since you don't have to worry about taxes. Outside of these tax shelters, rebalancing can trigger capital gains taxes. When looking at your investments, don't forget to include all of your assets together, your 401(k), IRAs, and other investments. Then, try to do any needed rebalancing within the nontaxable accounts, or take up to $3,000 (limited by tax law) in capital losses as a tax deduction in your taxable accounts. (Hopefully, you won't have any losses to take, but statistically speaking, the odds are you will someday. *All investments will go down at some point in time*. It's unavoidable.)

Don't Just Do Something, Sit There

Rebalance your portfolio just one time per year. Do not attempt to sell stock mutual funds because you believe the market is going lower. Do not attempt to buy stock mutual funds because you believe the market is going higher. This is referred to as market timing or timing the market. You might get it right once or even twice, but no one has ever come up with a reliable system for timing the market.

I personally know several folks that sold all of their stock funds as the market was falling in 2008. For several months these folks looked like geniuses as they avoided further losses. Unfortunately, being correct once can cost you a lot of money. Most of these people are still in cash or bonds, and they never bought back in to their stock mutual funds. Thus, while they saved themselves some money when the market was on the way down, the market quickly rose above the point where they had sold before they could even finish patting themselves on the back. The market has now nearly doubled (up 100%), and they are in no-man's-land because they missed the big rally. They were too afraid to buy back in after a 20 percent run in the market and kept waiting for a pullback, only to watch the market go nonstop up 50, 70, and now 100 percent. These folks will likely jump back in at exactly the wrong time.

Don't be that panicky investor that sells during market turmoil. Stay the course, and rebalance your portfolio once a year. You will eventually be forced to add to your stock mutual funds at a scary time when the market is down, and the economy looks bad. However, isn't the point of investing to buy low and sell high? Rebalance your portfolio once per year, and that is exactly what you will accomplish.

Investments *Outside* Your 401(k), IRA, or 403(b)

The recipes in this book represent typical portfolios I would recommend for tax-sheltered investments like 401(k), 403(b), TSP, or IRA. Modifications would need to be made for investors in high-income tax brackets regarding investments outside of tax-sheltered plans. Generally speaking, the high-tax-bracket investor would want to use tax-free municipal bond funds for bond investments that have to be held outside of a tax shelter. In addition, any investor who has both tax-sheltered investments and investments outside of tax shelters would want to hold tax-inefficient investments such as bond funds, small cap stock funds, and international stock funds within the tax shelter. The more tax-efficient large cap stock index funds could then be used for investments that are not inside a tax-sheltered plan.

If you are in a higher income tax bracket, you should consider substituting the bond ETFs in the recipes (which are all taxable) with the following alternatives (which are exempt from federal taxation in most cases):

ETF Examples (Ticker Symbol):
SPDR Nuveen Barclays Capital Short-Term Muni Bond ETF (SHM)
Market Vectors Intermediate Municipal Index ETF (ITM)
iShares S&P National Municipal Bond ETF (MUB)

or

Vanguard Mutual Fund Examples (Ticker Symbol):
Vanguard Short-Term Tax-Exempt Bond Fund (VWSTX)
Vanguard Intermediate-Term Tax-Exempt Bond Fund (VWITX)
Vanguard Long-Term Tax-Exempt Bond Fund (VWLTX)

Lastly, Vanguard also offers certain state specific tax-exempt bond funds that should be tax-exempt from both federal and state taxes for investors that live in these specific states: California, Florida, Massachusetts, New Jersey, New York, Ohio, and Pennsylvania.

The tax-exempt funds mentioned above should never be held within a tax-sheltered account like an IRA or 401(k) as the investor would be better off investing in the taxable bond funds in these accounts.

The example below shows a tax efficient portfolio. A large-cap stock index fund is quite tax efficient and is an excellent choice for a taxable investment account. In this example all the bond funds, that produce otherwise taxable interest payments, are held within tax deferred 401(k) and IRA accounts. Taxes will only be paid upon withdrawals from these two accounts.

The Tax Efficient Investor

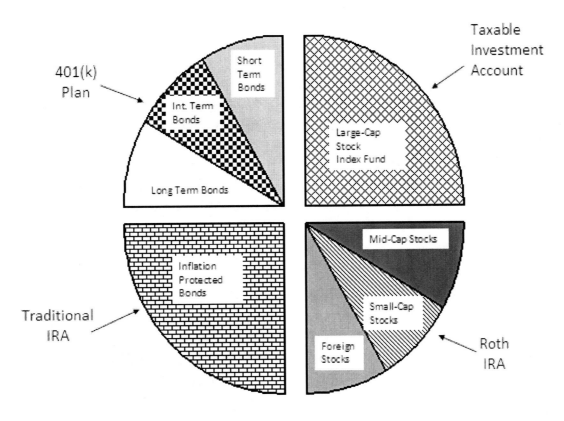

The Roth IRA is very special in that taxes will never need to be paid from withdrawals. Small-cap, mid-cap, and foreign stock funds are less tax efficient than large-cap stock index funds. Plus, these three asset classes have the highest potential returns. That makes these three asset classes perfect for a Roth IRA account.

REITs

Real Estate Investment Trusts, or REITs, have become popular investments. However, I see no reason to carve this industry out and declare it a necessary asset class for several reasons.

First, REITs are stocks that trade on the stock markets just like any other stock. So if you own an index fund (and you should), you already own REITs through that fund. I see no reason for you to own a separate fund that specifically owns REITs any more than you should own a separate fund that invests only in car companies or candy companies or gold miners or any other industry.

Second, if you own a bond fund, you already have a big exposure to real estate due to the fact that mortgage-backed bonds are roughly 35 percent of the bond market. So if you already own an indexed bond fund (and you should), you already have significant exposure to real estate.

Third, most folks' single biggest investment is their home. This is a big investment, but you are also levered, since you likely borrowed money to buy your home. I see no reason to add real estate exposure through REIT funds to any investor's portfolio.

Value vs. Growth

Many investment books will tell you to own a few value funds and a few growth funds for diversification. If you buy a large cap value fund and a large cap growth fund, you have created a large cap core portfolio by owning both of these. So simplify your portfolio, and just buy core funds (preferably index funds).

There have been studies that are famous in academic circles that suggest value stocks will beat growth stocks over the long term. However, the definition of value and growth differs from one mutual fund to the next. Nearly none define value and growth the way the most famous academic studies do.

The most popular stock indexes have value and growth styles. These style benchmarks needlessly reshuffle stocks from value to growth and back to value year after year. This just causes needless transaction costs for the relevant index funds that will result in long-term underperformance relative to the core indexes.

Commodities

Commodity funds that invest in metals or lumber have become popular recently, and they have been touted as good diversifiers and good hedges against inflation. Treasury Inflation Protected Securities (TIPS) are a far better hedge on inflation (and deflation). I have often said the price of my coffee table is uncorrelated to the stock market, but I'm not about to take 5 percent of my 401(k) or IRA and buy 100 coffee tables as a diversifying investment.

Plus, if you already own a diversified index fund (and you should), you already have exposure to companies that mine metals and harvest timber and make all the other commodities found in a commodity fund.

Just like I said with REITs, I see no reason to over leverage an investor to a specific industry that they already have exposure to via an index stock fund.

Company Stock

Some 401(k) plans offer your company's stock as an investment option. *Never* use this option if you are given a choice. This is the simple rule of "never put all your eggs in one basket." You do not want your current pay check *and* your retirement nest egg dependent on a single company. Think of all the employees at companies like, Enron, WorldCom, AIG, Lehman Brothers, and General Motors, who not only lost their jobs, but may have lost their entire 401(k) account if they had invested in company stock. Do not try to show your loyalty to your company by owning its stock within your 401(k). The risk is far too great.

Some companies that match your savings within a 401(k) account will match with company stock. Take that free money. But, sell that stock as soon as you are allowed – the time period may vary from plan to plan. Stay diversified and do not bet your current pay check and your retirement on a single company – even if you think you work for the best company on the planet.

I have personally known people who invested all of their 401(k) money in their company's stock. This is irresponsible and should not even be allowed by a 401(k) plan in my opinion. Unforeseen bad things can happen to any company at any time. You do not want to wake up one morning in your 50's and discover you are out of a job and your 401(k) account has gone to zero.

I have similar concerns regarding the G Fund in the Thrift Savings Plan. Your paycheck comes from the federal government; your pension depends on the government, your Social Security, and your medical care all depend on the federal government functioning properly. You may not want to also bet your personal savings on the same federal government that faces shut downs once or twice every year due to political standoffs when it comes to budgets and debt ceilings.

If you are forced to own company stock within your 401(k) plan, then you will need to slightly modify your investment recipe. For example, if company stock makes up 10 percent of your 401(k) account, then you will need to reduce your allocation to stock funds by that 10 percent figure. In this example, perhaps take 4 percent out of the large cap fund allocation, 3 percent from mid caps, 2 percent from small caps, and reduce your foreign stock allocation by 1 percent.

Passive Indexing Beats Active Management

Many studies have proven that active mutual fund managers (those that try to beat the market averages by buying only the stocks they think are the best) fail to beat passive buy-and-hold index funds. I'll highlight two studies below, but there are many to choose from.

A 15-year analysis of active mutual funds conducted by Robert Frick using data supplied by Morningstar and published in the September 2009 edition of *Kiplinger's Personal Finance Magazine* showed nearly 70 percent of active large cap mutual funds failed to beat the S&P 500 Index. The same analysis showed almost 90 percent of mid cap managers failed to beat the S&P MidCap 400 Index over the same 15-year period ending June 30, 2009.

Small cap managers and foreign stock managers performed somewhat better, as slightly more than half beat their passive benchmarks over 15 years. However, there also appeared to be evidence that even these markets were becoming more and more efficient, as less than half beat their benchmarks over the most recent 5-year period.

The Vanguard Investment Strategy Group studied the 10-year period from 1997–2007 and found that the average large cap core mutual fund underperformed passive indexes by an average of 1.7 percent per year. During the period large cap core mutual funds averaged an annual return of 4.4 percent versus the passive index return of 6.2 percent. In other words, active managers ate more than 25 percent of your returns during this period! Mid cap and small cap funds did somewhat better in this study, but they still underperformed their index on average.

The truth is that these studies actually *understate* just how bad mutual fund managers perform at picking stocks, and the odds are they will get only worse. Studies like these tend to suffer from what is called survivorship bias. The *Kiplinger* analysis is a backward-looking study that focused on just the funds in existence today and looked backward 15 years. Studies like this fail to capture the worst performing stock funds that go out of business or are merged into better performing funds. Sometimes the merger of two funds results in switching from one style box to another. For example, a large growth fund and a large value fund could merge and become a large core fund, and the new fund can keep whichever track record is better. This is a deplorable practice by mutual fund companies that allows them to bury their worst performing funds records.

During downturns in the stock market, it is common for actively managed funds to perform slightly better than in other market conditions. But this is also a mirage, and it is not a positive reflection on managers' stock-picking prowess. The fact is, mutual fund managers need to keep a portion of their funds assets in cash in order to meet investor withdrawals. During downturns in the stock market, high investor withdrawals can cause a manager to hold 5 percent cash or higher.

If the stock market falls 40 percent, as it did in 2008, and your fund manager brags it *only* lost 38 percent, don't let that fool you. The fund may have held 10 percent in cash, which means 90 percent of the fund held in stocks actually fell 44 percent!

As you are reading this, you are probably thinking to yourself, "But I won't buy average funds. I'll do some research and buy only the best funds that beat the markets." Unfortunately, it is extremely difficult to pick a winner.

It's Difficult to Pick Winners

A good place to research mutual funds is www.morningstar.com. However, just picking 5-star-rated mutual funds (Morningstar's highest rating) is not a sure path to success. The Burns Advisory Group studied 5-star funds going back to December 31, 1999, and discovered only 4 out of 248 5-star rated funds kept their 5-star rating after 10 years! What's worse is these 5-star rated funds underperformed their peers over the next 10 years.

In another study, the Vanguard Investment Strategy Group analyzed Lipper mutual fund returns data and found the top-performing funds in one period tend to become the worst-performing funds in the next time period. For example, the single best performing fund from 1987 to 1997 ranked just 6,656th from 1997 to 2007. In fact, 4 of the top 5 funds from 1987 to 1997 did not make the top 5,000 the following decade!

Thus, it is very easy to identify top-performing funds based on past performance, but it is much more difficult to pick a fund that will outperform *after* you buy it.

The Best Things in Life Are Free (Well, Almost)

The above analyses suggest investors should buy index funds whenever possible. This goes for bond funds as well as stock funds. Studies by Vanguard and Standard & Poor's and many others have shown bond fund managers are just as bad at beating passive benchmarks as the stock fund managers cited above. Luckily, index funds are plentiful and cheap (not quite free, but very close). There is no reason to pay a commission or sales fee or front-end load when buying index funds. And the expense ratios of the best index funds are 0.18 percent or even less.

That is as close to being free as you can get in the investment world. For these reasons, I've been a fan of Vanguard Mutual Funds for a long time, but there are good low-cost index funds at other fund companies, too. The Federal TSP has expenses lower than I've seen anywhere else at less than 0.03 percent!

Part 6

The Federal TSP

The Federal Employee's Thrift Savings Plan

The Thrift Savings Plan (TSP) is one of the best of all employee savings plans. What makes the plan great are its rock bottom expenses and simplicity. Another great aspect of the TSP is the generous matching funds available to *most* federal employees.

My only criticism of the TSP is that while matching funds are apparently available to almost all TSP participants, they are NOT available to our fighting men and women in the uniformed services. I think most Americans would be out right stunned to learn that our uniformed services are explicitly excluded from these extra funds.

I highly recommend everyone eligible for matching funds place a MINIMUM of 5 percent of every pay check into the TSP. The matching calculations are a bit complicated, but those lucky enough to be eligible for matching funds can maximize the generosity of the match by simply placing 5 percent of their pay into the TSP. With a 5 percent contribution, the match-eligible employee will receive an additional 5 percent of matching funds.

According to a survey by the Defined Contribution Institutional Investment Association, the proper savings rate for employees is 10 percent of your salary. That sounds about right to me - but only if you started early. If not, it should be even higher. The TSP makes getting to that 10 percent figure very easy for those eligible for matching funds. For a TSP participant in the 28 percent tax bracket, a pre-tax contribution to the TSP of 5 percent will only reduce the paycheck by 3.6 percent. Thus, by reducing your pay by only 3.6 percent, the employee can enjoy 10 percent going into the TSP.

Many 401(k) plans in private industry have high and often hidden expenses, but not so with the TSP where typical fund expenses are below 0.03% annually, likely the lowest investment expenses anywhere in the world.

Many 401(k) plans suffer from having too many choices. Some plans have good investment options, but an employee can get lost trying to find the good options when having to sift through so many bad options. It is not uncommon for a plan to have more than 20 different investment options. However, the TSP plan has just five basic funds to choose from and a few all-in-one funds that allocate among those five basic funds for the employee based on their anticipated retirement date.

I believe that the typical federal employee should use only four of these funds to create a solid portfolio:

C Fund (a large company stock index fund)
S Fund (a small company stock index fund)
I Fund (an international company stock index fund)
F Fund (a bond index fund)

The G Fund

The G Fund or Government Securities Investment Fund should be used sparingly and only after retirement has begun. The G Fund is the lowest risk investment option, but that also means it will provide the lowest long-term return. While trying to grow your TSP account before retirement, a TSP participant should avoid using this low return fund. In retirement, I recommend allocating no more than 20 percent of your total account to this fund. Remember, even in retirement, you are a long-term investor. If you are 75 years old, you must invest like you will live to be 100 – because you just might.

Contrary to its name, the G Fund or Government Securities Investment Fund does NOT buy marketable government securities. In the other 4 basic investment funds, the TSP takes your money and actually buys marketable investment securities in the form of stocks and bonds. This does NOT happen in the G Fund. It's not much more than a ledger book of IOUs to the TSP participants.

Stocks will beat bonds in the long-term, thus the investment recipes in this book allocate generously to the three stock based investment funds. Unfortunately, stocks do go down every few years. But, one can minimize the unpredictable stock downturns by owning bonds. Bonds usually rise in value when stocks go down. The F Fund fits this purpose very well, but the G Fund does NOT own any bonds and therefore does not provide the requisite ballast for your stock funds. While the G Fund is designed to never lose value, it does not rise in value the way the F Fund should when the stock funds (C, S, and I) go down.

The G Fund is a fantastic short-term bond fund. The G Fund will never fall in value and earns an investment return equal to a blended calculated rate of all outstanding government bonds with 4 or more years of maturity. **The G Fund is perhaps the best short-term investment fund ever invented, but it still is not appropriate for growing a retirement account with a long-term investment goal.**

As a federal employee with your salary, pension, and healthcare all dependent on the federal government, I do not recommend relying too heavily on the federal government within the TSP. We live in an age where the federal government is on the verge of shutting down every year during the annual budget negotiations where Democrats and Republicans play chicken with your paycheck. If you find yourself in a situation where your pay check or retirement check is late due to a government shut down, don't compound the problem by making the mistake of having all your TSP money locked in the G Fund.

Historical Performance

The S Fund and the I Fund were not actually launched until 2001. However, since 10 years is not a sufficiently long period of time to gauge long-term performance, I have inserted index returns as a proxy for how those two funds should have performed if they had been in existence in 1996.

	G	F	C	S	I
1996	6.8%	3.7%	22.9%	17.2%	0.6%
1997	6.8%	9.6%	33.2%	25.7%	-1.1%
1998	5.7%	8.7%	28.4%	8.6%	15.4%
1999	6.0%	-0.9%	21.0%	35.5%	29.3%
2000	6.4%	11.7%	-9.1%	-15.8%	-15.8%
2001	5.4%	8.6%	-11.9%	-9.0%	-21.9%
2002	5.0%	10.3%	-22.1%	-18.1%	-16.0%
2003	4.1%	4.1%	28.5%	42.9%	37.9%
2004	4.3%	4.3%	10.8%	18.0%	20.0%
2005	4.5%	2.4%	5.0%	10.5%	13.6%
2006	4.9%	4.4%	15.8%	15.3%	26.3%
2007	4.9%	7.1%	5.5%	5.5%	11.4%
2008	3.8%	5.5%	-37.0%	-38.3%	-42.4%
2009	3.0%	6.0%	26.7%	34.9%	30.0%
2010	2.8%	6.7%	15.1%	29.1%	7.9%

| 15-yr avg | 5.0% | 6.1% | 8.8% | 10.8% | 6.4% |

From the table above one can see that over a long period of time, one can expect that the G Fund will produce the lowest returns while the S Fund should produce the highest returns. Here are the funds ranked by the past 15 year average performance:

1. S Fund 10.8%
2. C Fund 8.8%
3. I Fund 6.4%
4. F Fund 6.1%
5. G Fund 5.0%

While performance from year to year can vary wildly, I expect the above rankings to continue going forward over long periods of time. Investors should not be tempted to put all their money in one single fund. While the G Fund is the safest fund, one can see it will likely provide the lowest return. Likewise, while the S Fund is expected to provide the highest long term returns, the year to year returns can fluctuate dramatically.

Notice in the table, that in the past 15 years the stock funds lost value in just 4 years. It is very important to also notice that in those years (2000, 2001, 2002, and 2008) the F Fund was the best performing fund and NOT the G Fund. Owning the three stock funds are crucial for long-term growth, while owning the F Fund is crucial for smoothing the ride during the unpredictable, yet inevitable downturns in the stock funds.

It would be great if one could anticipate the years when the stock funds will do poorly. Unfortunately no investment professional in history has ever been able to consistently predict the direction of the stock market from one year to the next. A patient investor that sticks with their prescribed investment recipe and annually rebalances their portfolio should do quite well over a long period of time.

The L Funds

The L Funds are all-in-one funds that allocate your money among the five basic funds for you. These are terrific funds in theory. Unfortunately all of the L Funds rely too heavily on allocations to the low risk, low returning G Fund. In fact, the L Funds are designed to increase the allocation to the G Fund dramatically over time, eventually placing a whooping 74 percent of your money into the G Fund! Since I recommend minimal usage of the G Fund, I must also recommend avoiding the L Funds.

Another reason to avoid the L Funds is that they only take into account one characteristic of the TSP participant – your expected retirement date. The L Funds do not incorporate any other characteristics that make every investor different. The 12 question quiz at the beginning of this book is designed to determine which allocation among the funds is best for you.

Part 7

How Much is Enough?

The Million Dollar Question

I am asked many questions. For example: "How much should I save each year?" "How much do I need to retire?" "Do I have enough to retire early?" "How much longer do I need to work?" "How much can I withdraw from my savings each year and not outlive my money?" "How do I bake a perfect brownie that is chewy, but not gooey?"

I can help you with all but the last question. In short, all of these questions boil down to:

How much is enough?

This is an amazingly complex question that is nearly impossible to answer. In order to truly know the answer to, "How much is enough," we need to consider dozens if not hundreds of variables that are not possible to know in advance.

When would you like to retire? Are you willing to work until you are 75? Perhaps you'd like to call it quits at 55 years old? How long are you going to live? Will you die at 60, 85, or perhaps live to be 100 years old? You should assume you will live to be 100 years old, or older. You don't want to run out of money when you are 80 years old. What would you do? Consider this, if you would like to retire at 55, this would mean you will work approximately 30-35 years. Thus, you would have approximately 30 years to earn enough money to support yourself for those 30 years *and* the next 50 years.

The Answer

Okay, you might want to sit down before you read the next sentence. If you want to live as comfortably in retirement as you do now, you may need to save 20-25 times your current annual salary! Think about what a daunting task that is! But, you can do it by starting to save early and following the recipes in this book.

Statistical analysis has shown that you should withdraw no more than 4-5 percent each year from your retirement savings. Anything higher than that and you might outlive your money. A simple example can illustrate why this leads to you needing to save 20-25 times your current salary if you want to live as comfortably in retirement as you do now.

An Example

Say your annual income is $45,000 per year and your spouse makes $55,000, for a total annual income of $100,000 per year. If you saved 22 times your annual salary, you would have $2.2 million. An annual withdrawal of 4.5 percent would equal $99,000.

You must consider what your expenses will be upon retirement. Most folks assume they can get by on less money in retirement than when they were working. That may or may not be true. Hopefully, you bought a house with a 30-year mortgage in your early 30's and will enjoy no longer having a house payment in your early 60's. In addition, you have been saving for retirement during your working years and not spending everything you make – at least I hope this is true.

Those two items will lower your expenses in retirement. However, have you thought about what you are going to do with yourself during the 40 hours per week that you used to be working? Most people want to enjoy their new spare time, but playing golf or many other hobbies can be quite expensive. Many people will chose to travel more extensively – perhaps to see old friends, sight seeing or visiting the grand kids. Perhaps you will need to pay for care givers as you get older?

Estimate Your Annual Expenses in Retirement

Let's get back to our example of the couple with $100,000 annual income. Perhaps they have a $1,000 per month mortgage payment and will make their final payment right before they retire. That is a $12,000 per year expense they will no longer incur. Thus, they could probably get by on $88,000 per year in retirement ($100,000-$12,000). Hopefully they have been setting aside money into their 401(k) plans at work all these years. Perhaps they have been putting away $15,000 per year – another expense they will not incur during retirement. Now, they figure they can get by on just $73,000 per year ($88,000-$15,000).

Further assume this couple plans to receive $24,000 per year in Social Security benefits. Now this couple seems to need just $49,000 per year to keep their current standard of living ($73,000-$24,000). Go to ssa.gov on the web and you can estimate your Social Security benefits.

Now instead of needing to save $2.2 million, they only need $1,078,000 (22 x $49,000). Let's further assume that both of these people are 50 years old and would like to retire at age 65. Our final assumption is that this couple has only been saving for the past 10 years, but since they have been putting $15,000 per year in their 401(k) plans, they now have amassed $225,000 in total savings. What will it take for this couple to reach their goal? Remember they want to achieve a balance of $1,078,000 which would allow them to safely withdraw $49,000 per year (roughly 4.5 percent per year withdrawal rate).

If you use the tables in the back of the book you will see that this couple would need to bump up their annual savings from their current rate of $15,000 per year to $16,500 per year and they can get very close to their goal.

The Tables

No one has a crystal ball and that requires us to make many assumptions or guesses. The following tables give you the ability to make educated guesses when trying to figure out how much you will have saved at retirement and how much you can withdraw each year.

Find the two pages that correspond to how many years until you would like to retire. To continue our example of the couple from above, go to the tables for "15 years until retirement."

Table A

In **Table A**, go down the left hand column to find the dollar amount you have already saved. In our example the couple had saved $225,000. Then slide across the columns until you come to one that approximates what you plan to save each year going forward. The number that is located at the intersection of your chosen row and column is a rough guess at how much money you will have accumulated by the time you want to retire.

In our continuing example, if you slide across the columns you will see that by beginning with $225,000 this couple would need to save $16,500 per year for the next 15 years to obtain a balance of $1,071,746 which is very close to their goal.

Your number in Table A may look quite large. However, you must keep in mind that you should only withdraw 4-5 percent each year while in retirement. This seemingly small withdrawal amount will keep you from outliving your money. If you retire earlier than 60, you should not withdraw more than 4 percent each year. Remember, you might live to be 100, or older. This nest egg may need to last a very long time.

Table B

In **Table B**, I have approximated how much you could safely withdraw from your corresponding figure in Table A. I have used an assumption of 4.5 percent annual withdrawal amount. If you retire earlier than 60 years old and are in good health, you should dial that figure down to just 4 percent. If you retire around 75, you could take out as much as 5 percent each year.

In our example, we found the 50-year old couple with $225,000 in savings could reach $1,071,746 by saving $16,500 per year for the next 15 years. If you now go to Table B, you will see that a 4.5% withdrawal rate will provide this couple $48,229 per year – very close to their needs of $49,000 per year.

In the tables I have used long-term return assumptions that are listed in the upper right hand corner. The longer you have until retirement, the higher the assumed rate of return on your investments. I assume you will follow the recipes in this book and will have more stock funds than bond funds early in life and will gradually move toward more bonds over time. Thus, I have lowered the assumed rate of return as you get closer and closer to retirement.

So how much should you set aside each year? You should strive to put the legal maximum amount in your 401(k) every year. If you can't save the legal maximum, save as much as you are able. For 2010 the maximum allowed by law is $22,000 for folks over 50 years old and $16,500 for everyone else. The legal maximum is adjusted each year for inflation. Go to irs.gov on the web to see what the new maximum amount is each year or ask your organization's benefits department. These figures are the maximum *you* contribute to a 401(k) plan and do *not* include any matching funds your organization might contribute.

In addition to saving in a 401(k) plan through your employer, you can contribute $5,000 each year (or $6,000 if you are over 50 years old) to an

IRA. If you are self-employed you should consult a tax professional to determine which type of retirement savings account is best for you, as there are a multitude of options that allow you to save significant amounts for retirement. For example, a SIMPLE IRA plan would allow contributions of up to $11,500 per year (or $14,000 for folks over 50); while a SEP IRA plan might allow you to sock away as much as $49,000 per year! I suggest consulting a CPA to determine which plan works best for your situation.

Time Value of Money (or, How to Buy a $30,000 Car for $23,000)

A dollar today is worth more than a dollar next year. Why? If you receive a dollar today, you can invest it for the next year at say, 4 percent interest. In one year you will have $1.04 instead of just one dollar. The difference is called the *time value of money*. There is something to be said for delayed gratification. There is likely no better example of this than the typical car purchase. If you are thinking of buying a new car, you may want to think again.

Consider the following example:

Say you agree to purchase a car for $24,700. Further, assume that the dealer arranges 5-year financing for you at a rate of 8 percent interest. Using a financial calculator one can figure that your monthly payment will be $500. Thus, the total true cost of the car can be calculated as 12 monthly payments of $500 for 5 years or $30,000 (60 payments x $500).

Wouldn't you love to purchase the car mentioned above for a true cost of $23,000 instead of $30,000? Of course you would, who wouldn't? Everyone can receive this discount. It just takes a little delayed gratification. Instead of purchasing the car today and paying the bank or financing company $500 each month, save that $500 and put it into a short-term bond mutual fund each and every month. If the bond fund returns just 4 percent per year, you will have accumulated $24,700 in less than 4 years (46 months to be exact).

Thus, the total true cost of the car would be just $23,000 (46 x $500). In both cases, the car dealer has agreed to sell you the car for the same $24,700 price. However, the difference in total cost to you is a whopping $7,000 ($30,000 - $23,000)! That $7,000 difference in the cost of a car is the difference between PAYING interest and EARNING interest.

Skip the Mocha and Retire Rich

I'd like to make a quick point for my younger readers. Earlier I went through an example of a couple that began saving $15,000 when they were 40 years old. This couple needed to boost their annual savings to $16,500 in order to retire with a smidge over $1 million. Perhaps you graduated from college at age 22 and immediately bought a new car with a 3-year loan and a $400 per month payment. Now you are 25 years old and you are thinking of buying another new car. Please don't do that. Instead, put that $400 per month into your 401(k) plan. If you look at the tables, you will see that if you invest just $400 per month ($4,800 per year) you could end up with roughly $1.3 million by the time you are ready to retire in 40 years at age 65. In other words, if you are young, you can retire a millionaire simply by putting the amount of a car payment into your 401(k) plan each month.

Better yet, a 25-year old should plan to work until 70 years old and then only needs to save $200 per month to amass $1 million. Think hard about this. If you are lucky enough to work for an organization that will match your savings dollar for dollar, you only need to put in $100 each month while your organization chips in another $100 and you can be a millionaire when you retire. And, don't forget that contributing to your 401(k) plan will reduce your taxes. So contributing $100 per month to your 401(k) plan will likely only reduce your pay check by only $80 each month.

Perhaps you stop at Starbucks to get an iced grande, non-fat no whip, black and white mocha for 4 bucks every day (Do *not* try this drink – it is addictive!). If you do this just five times a week, that's equal to roughly $80 per month. In other words, if you are young and work for a company with matching funds, you can retire a millionaire by simply putting the amount of a cup of coffee into your 401(k) plan each day. Skip the mocha and retire rich! Wow, that sounds like a good title for a book!

Matching Funds

If you are lucky and work for an organization that matches your savings in your 401(k) plan, then the *minimum* you should invest is whatever it takes to get the full matching funds available to you in your plan.

For example, if your organization will match 50 cents for every dollar you invest up to 6 percent of your salary, then the *minimum* you should invest is 6 percent. If matching funds are available, this is free money you should never pass up. This is a simple way to give yourself a raise in retirement.

Summary

Let's keep things simple. To the question, "How much is enough?" the answer is 22 times your annual expenses. To the question, "How much can I withdraw from my savings each year?" the answer is 4.5 percent. "How much should I save each year in my 401(k)?" The answer is you should strive to contribute the legal maximum of $22,000 if you are over 50 years old and $16,500 for everyone else. If your organization offers matching funds, *always* invest enough to receive the full matching funds available.

Part 8

The Tables

How much is enough?

Instructions for using the tables:

	Example:	You:
	15	

1. **Go to the page that is closest to the number of years before you hope to retire.**
   For example, if you are 50 and hope to retire at 65, then go to the page for 15 years until retirement.

2. **In Table A, go down the left hand column to the row that lists your total savings.**
   For example, perhaps you have $150,000 in your TSP and another $75,000 in an IRA.

   $ 225,000

3. **Slide over to the column with the amount you plan to save each year in the future.**
   Strive to invest the legal maximum each year ($22,000 in 2010 if older than 50, otherwise $16,500). Don't forget to add your matching funds (if applicable), and you can invest outside your TSP, too.

   $ 16,500

4. **This number guesstimates the amount you might accumulate by the time you retire.**
   For our example, we started with $225,000 and invested $16,500 per year for 15 years.

   $1,071,746

5. **Go to Table B (on the next page) and find the corresponding figure.**
   This figure represents the amount you could safely withdraw each year in retirement (4.5%). Remember, you will need to pay income tax on withdrawals from your TSP or traditional IRA.

   $ 48,229 *

6. **If the figure in #5 is less than you wish, you need to do one the following:**

   a. Save more each year (try moving over a few columns) and/or,
   b. Postpone retirement and work more years (try going to a different page) and/or,
   c. Plan to live more frugally in retirement.

* **Note:** The figures in the tables have not been adjusted for inflation. Your actual purchasing power will be eroded by inflation. In our example, the $48,229 would have a purchasing power of $30,956 in today's dollars if inflation averaged 3 percent per year for 15 years.

Years to Retirement: 0

Table A: The Future Value of Your Savings

	There is no need for Table A if you are in retirement. Go straight to Table B.

80

Years to Retirement: 0

Table B: The Amount You Could Safely Withdraw from Your Savings Each Year

Age →	40	50	60	65	70	75	80
Years in Retirement*	**60**	**50**	**40**	**35**	**30**	**25**	**20**
Safe Withdrawal Rate	3.50%	3.75%	4.00%	4.50%	4.75%	5.00%	5.25%
Savings Amount							
$ 10,000	$350	$375	$400	$450	$475	$500	$525
$ 25,000	$875	$938	$1,000	$1,125	$1,188	$1,250	$1,313
$ 50,000	$1,750	$1,875	$2,000	$2,250	$2,375	$2,500	$2,625
$ 75,000	$2,625	$2,813	$3,000	$3,375	$3,563	$3,750	$3,938
$ 100,000	$3,500	$3,750	$4,000	$4,500	$4,750	$5,000	$5,250
$ 125,000	$4,375	$4,688	$5,000	$5,625	$5,938	$6,250	$6,563
$ 150,000	$5,250	$5,625	$6,000	$6,750	$7,125	$7,500	$7,875
$ 200,000	$7,000	$7,500	$8,000	$9,000	$9,500	$10,000	$10,500
$ 250,000	$8,750	$9,375	$10,000	$11,250	$11,875	$12,500	$13,125
$ 300,000	$10,500	$11,250	$12,000	$13,500	$14,250	$15,000	$15,750
$ 350,000	$12,250	$13,125	$14,000	$15,750	$16,625	$17,500	$18,375
$ 400,000	$14,000	$15,000	$16,000	$18,000	$19,000	$20,000	$21,000
$ 450,000	$15,750	$16,875	$18,000	$20,250	$21,375	$22,500	$23,625
$ 500,000	$17,500	$18,750	$20,000	$22,500	$23,750	$25,000	$26,250
$ 600,000	$21,000	$22,500	$24,000	$27,000	$28,500	$30,000	$31,500
$ 700,000	$24,500	$26,250	$28,000	$31,500	$33,250	$35,000	$36,750
$ 800,000	$28,000	$30,000	$32,000	$36,000	$38,000	$40,000	$42,000
$ 900,000	$31,500	$33,750	$36,000	$40,500	$42,750	$45,000	$47,250
$ 1,000,000	$35,000	$37,500	$40,000	$45,000	$47,500	$50,000	$52,500
$ 1,250,000	$43,750	$46,875	$50,000	$56,250	$59,375	$62,500	$65,625
$ 1,500,000	$52,500	$56,250	$60,000	$67,500	$71,250	$75,000	$78,750
$ 1,750,000	$61,250	$65,625	$70,000	$78,750	$83,125	$87,500	$91,875
$ 2,000,000	$70,000	$75,000	$80,000	$90,000	$95,000	$100,000	$105,000
$ 3,000,000	$105,000	$112,500	$120,000	$135,000	$142,500	$150,000	$157,500

* You should plan to live 100 years, unless you have known medical problems.

Table A: The Future Value of Your Savings

| Additions: Monthly | $100 | $200 | $400 | $700 | $1,000 | $1,375 | $1,833 |
Yearly	$1,200	$2,400	$4,800	$8,400	$12,000	$16,500	$22,000
Current Balance							
$ -	$6,901	$13,802	$27,604	$48,306	$69,009	$94,887	$126,516
$ 10,000	$20,926	$27,827	$41,629	$62,332	$83,034	$108,913	$140,542
$ 20,000	$34,952	$41,853	$55,655	$76,357	$97,060	$122,938	$154,567
$ 30,000	$48,977	$55,878	$69,680	$90,383	$111,085	$136,964	$168,593
$ 40,000	$63,003	$69,904	$83,706	$104,408	$125,111	$150,989	$182,618
$ 50,000	$77,028	$83,929	$97,731	$118,434	$139,136	$165,015	$196,644
$ 60,000	$91,054	$97,955	$111,757	$132,459	$153,162	$179,040	$210,669
$ 70,000	$105,080	$111,980	$125,782	$146,485	$167,187	$193,066	$224,695
$ 80,000	$119,105	$126,006	$139,808	$160,510	$181,213	$207,091	$238,720
$ 90,000	$133,131	$140,031	$153,833	$174,536	$195,239	$221,117	$252,746
$ 100,000	$147,156	$154,057	$167,859	$188,561	$209,264	$235,142	$266,771
$ 125,000	$182,220	$189,121	$202,923	$223,625	$244,328	$270,206	$301,835
$ 150,000	$217,284	$224,185	$237,986	$258,689	$279,392	$305,270	$336,899
$ 175,000	$252,347	$259,248	$273,050	$293,753	$314,455	$340,334	$371,963
$ 200,000	$287,411	$294,312	$308,114	$328,817	$349,519	$375,398	$407,026
$ 225,000	$322,475	$329,376	$343,178	$363,880	$384,583	$410,461	$442,090
$ 250,000	$357,539	$364,440	$378,241	$398,944	$419,647	$445,525	$477,154
$ 300,000	$427,666	$434,567	$448,369	$469,072	$489,774	$515,653	$547,282
$ 350,000	$497,794	$504,695	$518,497	$539,199	$559,902	$585,780	$617,409
$ 400,000	$567,922	$574,822	$588,624	$609,327	$630,030	$655,908	$687,537
$ 500,000	$708,177	$715,078	$728,879	$749,582	$770,285	$796,163	$827,792
$ 750,000	$1,058,815	$1,065,716	$1,079,517	$1,100,220	$1,120,923	$1,146,801	$1,178,430
$ 1,000,000	$1,409,453	$1,416,354	$1,430,155	$1,450,858	$1,471,561	$1,497,439	$1,529,068
$ 2,000,000	$2,812,004	$2,818,905	$2,832,707	$2,853,410	$2,874,112	$2,899,991	$2,931,619

Years to Retirement: 5

Annual Withdrawal Percentage: 4.5%

Table B: The Amount You Could Safely Withdraw from Your Savings Each Year

Additions: Monthly		$100	$200	$400	$700	$1,000	$1,375	$1,833
Yearly		$1,200	$2,400	$4,800	$8,400	$12,000	$16,500	$22,000
Current Balance								
$ -		$311	$621	$1,242	$2,174	$3,105	$4,270	$5,693
$ 10,000		$942	$1,252	$1,873	$2,805	$3,737	$4,901	$6,324
$ 20,000		$1,573	$1,883	$2,504	$3,436	$4,368	$5,532	$6,956
$ 30,000		$2,204	$2,515	$3,136	$4,067	$4,999	$6,163	$7,587
$ 40,000		$2,835	$3,146	$3,767	$4,698	$5,630	$6,795	$8,218
$ 50,000		$3,466	$3,777	$4,398	$5,330	$6,261	$7,426	$8,849
$ 60,000		$4,097	$4,408	$5,029	$5,961	$6,892	$8,057	$9,480
$ 70,000		$4,729	$5,039	$5,660	$6,592	$7,523	$8,688	$10,111
$ 80,000		$5,360	$5,670	$6,291	$7,223	$8,155	$9,319	$10,742
$ 90,000		$5,991	$6,301	$6,922	$7,854	$8,786	$9,950	$11,374
$ 100,000		$6,622	$6,933	$7,554	$8,485	$9,417	$10,581	$12,005
$ 125,000		$8,200	$8,510	$9,132	$10,063	$10,995	$12,159	$13,583
$ 150,000		$9,778	$10,088	$10,709	$11,641	$12,573	$13,737	$15,160
$ 175,000		$11,356	$11,666	$12,287	$13,219	$14,150	$15,315	$16,738
$ 200,000		$12,934	$13,244	$13,865	$14,797	$15,728	$16,893	$18,316
$ 225,000		$14,511	$14,822	$15,443	$16,375	$17,306	$18,471	$19,894
$ 250,000		$16,089	$16,400	$17,021	$17,952	$18,884	$20,049	$21,472
$ 300,000		$19,245	$19,556	$20,177	$21,108	$22,040	$23,204	$24,628
$ 350,000		$22,401	$22,711	$23,332	$24,264	$25,196	$26,360	$27,783
$ 400,000		$25,556	$25,867	$26,488	$27,420	$28,351	$29,516	$30,939
$ 500,000		$31,868	$32,178	$32,800	$33,731	$34,663	$35,827	$37,251
$ 750,000		$47,647	$47,957	$48,578	$49,510	$50,442	$51,606	$53,029
$ 1,000,000		$63,425	$63,736	$64,357	$65,289	$66,220	$67,385	$68,808
$ 2,000,000		$126,540	$126,851	$127,472	$128,403	$129,335	$130,500	$131,923

Table A: The Future Value of Your Savings

| Additions: Monthly | $100 | $200 | $400 | $700 | $1,000 | $1,375 | $1,833 |
Yearly	$1,200	$2,400	$4,800	$8,400	$12,000	$16,500	$22,000
Current Balance							
$ -	$16,737	$33,474	$66,949	$117,160	$167,372	$230,136	$306,848
$ 10,000	$36,780	$53,517	$86,991	$137,203	$187,414	$250,179	$326,890
$ 20,000	$56,822	$73,559	$107,033	$157,245	$207,457	$270,221	$346,933
$ 30,000	$76,864	$93,601	$127,076	$177,287	$227,499	$290,263	$366,975
$ 40,000	$96,906	$113,644	$147,118	$197,330	$247,541	$310,306	$387,017
$ 50,000	$116,949	$133,686	$167,160	$217,372	$267,583	$330,348	$407,059
$ 60,000	$136,991	$153,728	$187,203	$237,414	$287,626	$350,390	$427,102
$ 70,000	$157,033	$173,771	$207,245	$257,457	$307,668	$370,433	$447,144
$ 80,000	$177,076	$193,813	$227,287	$277,499	$327,710	$390,475	$467,186
$ 90,000	$197,118	$213,855	$247,330	$297,541	$347,753	$410,517	$487,229
$ 100,000	$217,160	$233,898	$267,372	$317,583	$367,795	$430,559	$507,271
$ 125,000	$267,266	$284,003	$317,478	$367,689	$417,901	$480,665	$557,377
$ 150,000	$317,372	$334,109	$367,583	$417,795	$468,007	$530,771	$607,483
$ 175,000	$367,478	$384,215	$417,689	$467,901	$518,112	$580,877	$657,588
$ 200,000	$417,583	$434,321	$467,795	$518,007	$568,218	$630,983	$707,694
$ 225,000	$467,689	$484,426	$517,901	$568,112	$618,324	$681,088	$757,800
$ 250,000	$517,795	$534,532	$568,007	$618,218	$668,430	$731,194	$807,906
$ 300,000	$618,007	$634,744	$668,218	$718,430	$768,641	$831,406	$908,117
$ 350,000	$718,218	$734,955	$768,430	$818,641	$868,853	$931,617	$1,008,329
$ 400,000	$818,430	$835,167	$868,641	$918,853	$969,064	$1,031,829	$1,108,540
$ 500,000	$1,018,853	$1,035,590	$1,069,064	$1,119,276	$1,169,488	$1,232,252	$1,308,964
$ 750,000	$1,519,911	$1,536,648	$1,570,122	$1,620,334	$1,670,545	$1,733,310	$1,810,021
$1,000,000	$2,020,969	$2,037,706	$2,071,180	$2,121,392	$2,171,603	$2,234,368	$2,311,079
$2,000,000	$4,025,200	$4,041,937	$4,075,411	$4,125,623	$4,175,835	$4,238,599	$4,315,311

Years to Retirement: 10

Annual Withdrawal Percentage: 4.5%

Table B: The Amount You Could Safely Withdraw from Your Savings Each Year

| Additions: Monthly | $100 | $200 | $400 | $700 | $1,000 | $1,375 | $1,833 |
Yearly	$1,200	$2,400	$4,800	$8,400	$12,000	$16,500	$22,000
Current Balance							
$ -	$753	$1,506	$3,013	$5,272	$7,532	$10,356	$13,808
$ 10,000	$1,655	$2,408	$3,915	$6,174	$8,434	$11,258	$14,710
$ 20,000	$2,557	$3,310	$4,817	$7,076	$9,336	$12,160	$15,612
$ 30,000	$3,459	$4,212	$5,718	$7,978	$10,237	$13,062	$16,514
$ 40,000	$4,361	$5,114	$6,620	$8,880	$11,139	$13,964	$17,416
$ 50,000	$5,263	$6,016	$7,522	$9,782	$12,041	$14,866	$18,318
$ 60,000	$6,165	$6,918	$8,424	$10,684	$12,943	$15,768	$19,220
$ 70,000	$7,067	$7,820	$9,326	$11,586	$13,845	$16,669	$20,121
$ 80,000	$7,968	$8,722	$10,228	$12,487	$14,747	$17,571	$21,023
$ 90,000	$8,870	$9,623	$11,130	$13,389	$15,649	$18,473	$21,925
$ 100,000	$9,772	$10,525	$12,032	$14,291	$16,551	$19,375	$22,827
$ 125,000	$12,027	$12,780	$14,286	$16,546	$18,806	$21,630	$25,082
$ 150,000	$14,282	$15,035	$16,541	$18,801	$21,060	$23,885	$27,337
$ 175,000	$16,536	$17,290	$18,796	$21,056	$23,315	$26,139	$29,591
$ 200,000	$18,791	$19,544	$21,051	$23,310	$25,570	$28,394	$31,846
$ 225,000	$21,046	$21,799	$23,306	$25,565	$27,825	$30,649	$34,101
$ 250,000	$23,301	$24,054	$25,560	$27,820	$30,079	$32,904	$36,356
$ 300,000	$27,810	$28,563	$30,070	$32,329	$34,589	$37,413	$40,865
$ 350,000	$32,320	$33,073	$34,579	$36,839	$39,098	$41,923	$45,375
$ 400,000	$36,829	$37,583	$39,089	$41,348	$43,608	$46,432	$49,884
$ 500,000	$45,848	$46,602	$48,108	$50,367	$52,627	$55,451	$58,903
$ 750,000	$68,396	$69,149	$70,656	$72,915	$75,175	$77,999	$81,451
$1,000,000	$90,944	$91,697	$93,203	$95,463	$97,722	$100,547	$103,999
$2,000,000	$181,134	$181,887	$183,394	$185,653	$187,913	$190,737	$194,189

Years to Retirement: 15

Annualized Return Guesstimate: 7.3%

Table A: The Future Value of Your Savings

Additions: Monthly	$100	$200	$400	$700	$1,000	$1,375	$1,833
Yearly	$1,200	$2,400	$4,800	$8,400	$12,000	$16,500	$22,000
Current Balance							
$ -	$30,861	$61,722	$123,444	$216,026	$308,609	$424,337	$565,782
$ 10,000	$59,635	$90,495	$152,217	$244,800	$337,383	$453,111	$594,556
$ 20,000	$88,408	$119,269	$180,991	$273,574	$366,156	$481,885	$623,329
$ 30,000	$117,182	$148,043	$209,765	$302,347	$394,930	$510,658	$652,103
$ 40,000	$145,956	$176,817	$238,538	$331,121	$423,704	$539,432	$680,877
$ 50,000	$174,729	$205,590	$267,312	$359,895	$452,477	$568,206	$709,650
$ 60,000	$203,503	$234,364	$296,086	$388,668	$481,251	$596,979	$738,424
$ 70,000	$232,277	$263,138	$324,860	$417,442	$510,025	$625,753	$767,198
$ 80,000	$261,051	$291,911	$353,633	$446,216	$538,799	$654,527	$795,972
$ 90,000	$289,824	$320,685	$382,407	$474,990	$567,572	$683,301	$824,745
$ 100,000	$318,598	$349,459	$411,181	$503,763	$596,346	$712,074	$853,519
$ 125,000	$390,532	$421,393	$483,115	$575,698	$668,280	$784,009	$925,453
$ 150,000	$462,467	$493,327	$555,049	$647,632	$740,215	$855,943	$997,388
$ 175,000	$534,401	$565,262	$626,983	$719,566	$812,149	$927,877	$1,069,322
$ 200,000	$606,335	$637,196	$698,918	$791,500	$884,083	$999,811	$1,141,256
$ 225,000	$678,269	$709,130	$770,852	$863,435	$956,017	**$1,071,746**	$1,213,190
$ 250,000	$750,204	$781,064	$842,786	$935,369	$1,027,952	$1,143,680	$1,285,125
$ 300,000	$894,072	$924,933	$986,655	$1,079,237	$1,171,820	$1,287,548	$1,428,993
$ 350,000	$1,037,941	$1,068,802	$1,130,523	$1,223,106	$1,315,689	$1,431,417	$1,572,862
$ 400,000	$1,181,809	$1,212,670	$1,274,392	$1,366,975	$1,459,557	$1,575,286	$1,716,730
$ 500,000	$1,469,546	$1,500,407	$1,562,129	$1,654,712	$1,747,294	$1,863,023	$2,004,467
$ 750,000	$2,188,889	$2,219,750	$2,281,472	$2,374,054	$2,466,637	$2,582,365	$2,723,810
$ 1,000,000	$2,908,232	$2,939,093	$3,000,814	$3,093,397	$3,185,980	$3,301,708	$3,443,153
$ 2,000,000	$5,785,602	$5,816,463	$5,878,185	$5,970,768	$6,063,350	$6,179,079	$6,320,524

Years to Retirement: 15

Annual Withdrawal Percentage: 4.5%

Table B: The Amount You Could Safely Withdraw from Your Savings Each Year

| Additions: Monthly | $100 | $200 | $400 | $700 | $1,000 | $1,375 | $1,833 |
Yearly	$1,200	$2,400	$4,800	$8,400	$12,000	$16,500	$22,000
Current Balance							
$ -	$1,389	$2,777	$5,555	$9,721	$13,887	$19,095	$25,460
$ 10,000	$2,684	$4,072	$6,850	$11,016	$15,182	$20,390	$26,755
$ 20,000	$3,978	$5,367	$8,145	$12,311	$16,477	$21,685	$28,050
$ 30,000	$5,273	$6,662	$9,439	$13,606	$17,772	$22,980	$29,345
$ 40,000	$6,568	$7,957	$10,734	$14,900	$19,067	$24,274	$30,639
$ 50,000	$7,863	$9,252	$12,029	$16,195	$20,361	$25,569	$31,934
$ 60,000	$9,158	$10,546	$13,324	$17,490	$21,656	$26,864	$33,229
$ 70,000	$10,452	$11,841	$14,619	$18,785	$22,951	$28,159	$34,524
$ 80,000	$11,747	$13,136	$15,913	$20,080	$24,246	$29,454	$35,819
$ 90,000	$13,042	$14,431	$17,208	$21,375	$25,541	$30,749	$37,114
$ 100,000	$14,337	$15,726	$18,503	$22,669	$26,836	$32,043	$38,408
$ 125,000	$17,574	$18,963	$21,740	$25,906	$30,073	$35,280	$41,645
$ 150,000	$20,811	$22,200	$24,977	$29,143	$33,310	$38,517	$44,882
$ 175,000	$24,048	$25,437	$28,214	$32,380	$36,547	$41,754	$48,119
$ 200,000	$27,285	$28,674	$31,451	$35,618	$39,784	$44,992	$51,357
$ 225,000	$30,522	$31,911	$34,688	$38,855	$43,021	**$48,229**	$54,594
$ 250,000	$33,759	$35,148	$37,925	$42,092	$46,258	$51,466	$57,831
$ 300,000	$40,233	$41,622	$44,399	$48,566	$52,732	$57,940	$64,305
$ 350,000	$46,707	$48,096	$50,874	$55,040	$59,206	$64,414	$70,779
$ 400,000	$53,181	$54,570	$57,348	$61,514	$65,680	$70,888	$77,253
$ 500,000	$66,130	$67,518	$70,296	$74,462	$78,628	$83,836	$90,201
$ 750,000	$98,500	$99,889	$102,666	$106,832	$110,999	$116,206	$122,571
$ 1,000,000	$130,870	$132,259	$135,037	$139,203	$143,369	$148,577	$154,942
$ 2,000,000	$260,352	$261,741	$264,518	$268,685	$272,851	$278,059	$284,424

Years to Retirement: 20   Annualized Return Guesstimate: 7.5%

Table A: The Future Value of Your Savings

Additions: Monthly → Yearly →	$100 $1,200	$200 $2,400	$400 $4,800	$700 $8,400	$1,000 $12,000	$1,375 $16,500	$1,833 $22,000
Current Balance							
$ -	$51,966	$103,931	$207,862	$363,759	$519,656	$714,527	$952,701
$ 10,000	$94,444	$146,410	$250,341	$406,238	$562,135	$757,006	$995,180
$ 20,000	$136,923	$188,888	$292,819	$448,716	$604,613	$799,484	$1,037,658
$ 30,000	$179,401	$231,367	$335,298	$491,195	$647,092	$841,963	$1,080,137
$ 40,000	$221,880	$273,845	$377,777	$533,673	$689,570	$884,441	$1,122,615
$ 50,000	$264,358	$316,324	$420,255	$576,152	$732,049	$926,920	$1,165,094
$ 60,000	$306,837	$358,802	$462,734	$618,630	$774,527	$969,398	$1,207,572
$ 70,000	$349,315	$401,281	$505,212	$661,109	$817,006	$1,011,877	$1,250,051
$ 80,000	$391,794	$443,759	$547,691	$703,587	$859,484	$1,054,355	$1,292,529
$ 90,000	$434,272	$486,238	$590,169	$746,066	$901,963	$1,096,834	$1,335,008
$ 100,000	$476,751	$528,716	$632,648	$788,544	$944,441	$1,139,312	$1,377,486
$ 125,000	$582,947	$634,913	$738,844	$894,741	$1,050,638	$1,245,509	$1,483,683
$ 150,000	$689,143	$741,109	$845,040	$1,000,937	$1,156,834	$1,351,705	$1,589,879
$ 175,000	$795,340	$847,305	$951,236	$1,107,133	$1,263,030	$1,457,901	$1,696,075
$ 200,000	$901,536	$953,501	$1,057,433	$1,213,330	$1,369,226	$1,564,097	$1,802,271
$ 225,000	$1,007,732	$1,059,698	$1,163,629	$1,319,526	$1,475,423	$1,670,294	$1,908,468
$ 250,000	$1,113,928	$1,165,894	$1,269,825	$1,425,722	$1,581,619	$1,776,490	$2,014,664
$ 300,000	$1,326,321	$1,378,287	$1,482,218	$1,638,115	$1,794,012	$1,988,883	$2,227,057
$ 350,000	$1,538,714	$1,590,679	$1,694,610	$1,850,507	$2,006,404	$2,201,275	$2,439,449
$ 400,000	$1,751,106	$1,803,072	$1,907,003	$2,062,900	$2,218,797	$2,413,668	$2,651,842
$ 500,000	$2,175,891	$2,227,857	$2,331,788	$2,487,685	$2,643,582	$2,838,453	$3,076,627
$ 750,000	$3,237,854	$3,289,820	$3,393,751	$3,549,648	$3,705,545	$3,900,416	$4,138,590
$1,000,000	$4,299,817	$4,351,782	$4,455,714	$4,611,610	$4,767,507	$4,962,378	$5,200,552
$2,000,000	$8,547,668	$8,599,633	$8,703,565	$8,859,462	$9,015,358	$9,210,229	$9,448,403

Years to Retirement: 20

Annual Withdrawal Percentage: 4.5%

Table B: The Amount You Could Safely Withdraw from Your Savings Each Year

Additions: Monthly	$100	$200	$400	$700	$1,000	$1,375	$1,833
Yearly	$1,200	$2,400	$4,800	$8,400	$12,000	$16,500	$22,000
Current Balance							
$ -	$2,338	$4,677	$9,354	$16,369	$23,385	$32,154	$42,872
$ 10,000	$4,250	$6,588	$11,265	$18,281	$25,296	$34,065	$44,783
$ 20,000	$6,162	$8,500	$13,177	$20,192	$27,208	$35,977	$46,695
$ 30,000	$8,073	$10,412	$15,088	$22,104	$29,119	$37,888	$48,606
$ 40,000	$9,985	$12,323	$17,000	$24,015	$31,031	$39,800	$50,518
$ 50,000	$11,896	$14,235	$18,911	$25,927	$32,942	$41,711	$52,429
$ 60,000	$13,808	$16,146	$20,823	$27,838	$34,854	$43,623	$54,341
$ 70,000	$15,719	$18,058	$22,735	$29,750	$36,765	$45,534	$56,252
$ 80,000	$17,631	$19,969	$24,646	$31,661	$38,677	$47,446	$58,164
$ 90,000	$19,542	$21,881	$26,558	$33,573	$40,588	$49,358	$60,075
$ 100,000	$21,454	$23,792	$28,469	$35,484	$42,500	$51,269	$61,987
$ 125,000	$26,233	$28,571	$33,248	$40,263	$47,279	$56,048	$66,766
$ 150,000	$31,011	$33,350	$38,027	$45,042	$52,058	$60,827	$71,545
$ 175,000	$35,790	$38,129	$42,806	$49,821	$56,836	$65,606	$76,323
$ 200,000	$40,569	$42,908	$47,584	$54,600	$61,615	$70,384	$81,102
$ 225,000	$45,348	$47,686	$52,363	$59,379	$66,394	$75,163	$85,881
$ 250,000	$50,127	$52,465	$57,142	$64,157	$71,173	$79,942	$90,660
$ 300,000	$59,684	$62,023	$66,700	$73,715	$80,731	$89,500	$100,218
$ 350,000	$69,242	$71,581	$76,257	$83,273	$90,288	$99,057	$109,775
$ 400,000	$78,800	$81,138	$85,815	$92,830	$99,846	$108,615	$119,333
$ 500,000	$97,915	$100,254	$104,930	$111,946	$118,961	$127,730	$138,448
$ 750,000	$145,703	$148,042	$152,719	$159,734	$166,750	$175,519	$186,237
$ 1,000,000	$193,492	$195,830	$200,507	$207,522	$214,538	$223,307	$234,025
$ 2,000,000	$384,645	$386,984	$391,660	$398,676	$405,691	$414,460	$425,178

Years to Retirement: 25

Table A: The Future Value of Your Savings

| Additions: Monthly | $100 | $200 | $400 | $700 | $1,000 | $1,375 | $1,833 |
Yearly	$1,200	$2,400	$4,800	$8,400	$12,000	$16,500	$22,000
Current Balance							
$ -	$82,765	$165,529	$331,058	$579,352	$827,646	$1,138,013	$1,517,348
$ 10,000	$145,182	$227,947	$393,476	$641,770	$890,063	$1,200,430	$1,579,765
$ 20,000	$207,600	$290,364	$455,893	$704,187	$952,481	$1,262,848	$1,642,183
$ 30,000	$270,017	$352,782	$518,311	$766,605	$1,014,898	$1,325,265	$1,704,600
$ 40,000	$332,435	$415,199	$580,729	$829,022	$1,077,316	$1,387,683	$1,767,018
$ 50,000	$394,852	$477,617	$643,146	$891,440	$1,139,733	$1,450,101	$1,829,435
$ 60,000	$457,270	$540,034	$705,564	$953,857	$1,202,151	$1,512,518	$1,891,853
$ 70,000	$519,687	$602,452	$767,981	$1,016,275	$1,264,569	$1,574,936	$1,954,271
$ 80,000	$582,105	$664,870	$830,399	$1,078,692	$1,326,986	$1,637,353	$2,016,688
$ 90,000	$644,523	$727,287	$892,816	$1,141,110	$1,389,404	$1,699,771	$2,079,106
$ 100,000	$706,940	$789,705	$955,234	$1,203,528	$1,451,821	$1,762,188	$2,141,523
$ 125,000	$862,984	$945,749	$1,111,278	$1,359,571	$1,607,865	$1,918,232	$2,297,567
$ 150,000	$1,019,028	$1,101,793	$1,267,322	$1,515,615	$1,763,909	$2,074,276	$2,453,611
$ 175,000	$1,175,072	$1,257,836	$1,423,366	$1,671,659	$1,919,953	$2,230,320	$2,609,655
$ 200,000	$1,331,116	$1,413,880	$1,579,409	$1,827,703	$2,075,997	$2,386,364	$2,765,699
$ 225,000	$1,487,160	$1,569,924	$1,735,453	$1,983,747	$2,232,041	$2,542,408	$2,921,743
$ 250,000	$1,643,204	$1,725,968	$1,891,497	$2,139,791	$2,388,085	$2,698,452	$3,077,787
$ 300,000	$1,955,291	$2,038,056	$2,203,585	$2,451,879	$2,700,172	$3,010,540	$3,389,874
$ 350,000	$2,267,379	$2,350,144	$2,515,673	$2,763,967	$3,012,260	$3,322,627	$3,701,962
$ 400,000	$2,579,467	$2,662,232	$2,827,761	$3,076,054	$3,324,348	$3,634,715	$4,014,050
$ 500,000	$3,203,643	$3,286,407	$3,451,936	$3,700,230	$3,948,524	$4,258,891	$4,638,226
$ 750,000	$4,764,082	$4,846,846	$5,012,375	$5,260,669	$5,508,963	$5,819,330	$6,198,665
$1,000,000	$6,324,521	$6,407,285	$6,572,814	$6,821,108	$7,069,402	$7,379,769	$7,759,104
$2,000,000	$12,566,276	$12,649,041	$12,814,570	$13,062,864	$13,311,158	$13,621,525	$14,000,860

Years to Retirement: 25

Annual Withdrawal Percentage: 4.5%

Table B: The Amount You Could Safely Withdraw from Your Savings Each Year

| Additions: Monthly | $100 | $200 | $400 | $700 | $1,000 | $1,375 | $1,833 |
Yearly	$1,200	$2,400	$4,800	$8,400	$12,000	$16,500	$22,000
Current Balance							
$ -	$3,724	$7,449	$14,898	$26,071	$37,244	$51,211	$68,281
$ 10,000	$6,533	$10,258	$17,706	$28,880	$40,053	$54,019	$71,089
$ 20,000	$9,342	$13,066	$20,515	$31,688	$42,862	$56,828	$73,898
$ 30,000	$12,151	$15,875	$23,324	$34,497	$45,670	$59,637	$76,707
$ 40,000	$14,960	$18,684	$26,133	$37,306	$48,479	$62,446	$79,516
$ 50,000	$17,768	$21,493	$28,942	$40,115	$51,288	$65,255	$82,325
$ 60,000	$20,577	$24,302	$31,750	$42,924	$54,097	$68,063	$85,133
$ 70,000	$23,386	$27,110	$34,559	$45,732	$56,906	$70,872	$87,942
$ 80,000	$26,195	$29,919	$37,368	$48,541	$59,714	$73,681	$90,751
$ 90,000	$29,004	$32,728	$40,177	$51,350	$62,523	$76,490	$93,560
$ 100,000	$31,812	$35,537	$42,986	$54,159	$65,332	$79,298	$96,369
$ 125,000	$38,834	$42,559	$50,007	$61,181	$72,354	$86,320	$103,391
$ 150,000	$45,856	$49,581	$57,029	$68,203	$79,376	$93,342	$110,412
$ 175,000	$52,878	$56,603	$64,051	$75,225	$86,398	$100,364	$117,434
$ 200,000	$59,900	$63,625	$71,073	$82,247	$93,420	$107,386	$124,456
$ 225,000	$66,922	$70,647	$78,095	$89,269	$100,442	$114,408	$131,478
$ 250,000	$73,944	$77,669	$85,117	$96,291	$107,464	$121,430	$138,500
$ 300,000	$87,988	$91,713	$99,161	$110,335	$121,508	$135,474	$152,544
$ 350,000	$102,032	$105,756	$113,205	$124,378	$135,552	$149,518	$166,588
$ 400,000	$116,076	$119,800	$127,249	$138,422	$149,596	$163,562	$180,632
$ 500,000	$144,164	$147,888	$155,337	$166,510	$177,684	$191,650	$208,720
$ 750,000	$214,384	$218,108	$225,557	$236,730	$247,903	$261,870	$278,940
$ 1,000,000	$284,603	$288,328	$295,777	$306,950	$318,123	$332,090	$349,160
$ 2,000,000	$565,482	$569,207	$576,656	$587,829	$599,002	$612,969	$630,039

Years to Retirement: 30   Annualized Return Guesstimate: 7.8%

Table A: The Future Value of Your Savings

Additions: Monthly / Yearly	$100 / $1,200	$200 / $2,400	$400 / $4,800	$700 / $8,400	$1,000 / $12,000	$1,375 / $16,500	$1,833 / $22,000
Current Balance							
$ -	$131,052	$262,104	$524,208	$917,363	$1,310,519	$1,801,964	$2,402,614
$ 10,000	$226,236	$357,288	$619,391	$1,012,547	$1,405,703	$1,897,148	$2,497,798
$ 20,000	$321,419	$452,471	$714,575	$1,107,731	$1,500,887	$1,992,332	$2,592,982
$ 30,000	$416,603	$547,655	$809,759	$1,202,915	$1,596,071	$2,087,515	$2,688,166
$ 40,000	$511,787	$642,839	$904,943	$1,298,099	$1,691,254	$2,182,699	$2,783,349
$ 50,000	$606,971	$738,023	$1,000,126	$1,393,282	$1,786,438	$2,277,883	$2,878,533
$ 60,000	$702,154	$833,206	$1,095,310	$1,488,466	$1,881,622	$2,373,067	$2,973,717
$ 70,000	$797,338	$928,390	$1,190,494	$1,583,650	$1,976,806	$2,468,250	$3,068,901
$ 80,000	$892,522	$1,023,574	$1,285,678	$1,678,834	$2,071,989	$2,563,434	$3,164,084
$ 90,000	$987,706	$1,118,758	$1,380,861	$1,774,017	$2,167,173	$2,658,618	$3,259,268
$ 100,000	$1,082,889	$1,213,941	$1,476,045	$1,869,201	$2,262,357	$2,753,802	$3,354,452
$ 125,000	$1,320,849	$1,451,901	$1,714,005	$2,107,160	$2,500,316	$2,991,761	$3,592,411
$ 150,000	$1,558,808	$1,689,860	$1,951,964	$2,345,120	$2,738,276	$3,229,720	$3,830,371
$ 175,000	$1,796,768	$1,927,820	$2,189,923	$2,583,079	$2,976,235	$3,467,680	$4,068,330
$ 200,000	$2,034,727	$2,165,779	$2,427,883	$2,821,039	$3,214,194	$3,705,639	$4,306,289
$ 225,000	$2,272,686	$2,403,738	$2,665,842	$3,058,998	$3,452,154	$3,943,598	$4,544,249
$ 250,000	$2,510,646	$2,641,698	$2,903,802	$3,296,957	$3,690,113	$4,181,558	$4,782,208
$ 300,000	$2,986,565	$3,117,616	$3,379,720	$3,772,876	$4,166,032	$4,657,477	$5,258,127
$ 350,000	$3,462,483	$3,593,535	$3,855,639	$4,248,795	$4,641,951	$5,133,395	$5,734,046
$ 400,000	$3,938,402	$4,069,454	$4,331,558	$4,724,714	$5,117,869	$5,609,314	$6,209,964
$ 500,000	$4,890,240	$5,021,292	$5,283,395	$5,676,551	$6,069,707	$6,561,152	$7,161,802
$ 750,000	$7,269,833	$7,400,885	$7,662,989	$8,056,145	$8,449,301	$8,940,746	$9,541,396
$ 1,000,000	$9,649,427	$9,780,479	$10,042,583	$10,435,739	$10,828,895	$11,320,339	$11,920,990
$ 2,000,000	$19,167,803	$19,298,854	$19,560,958	$19,954,114	$20,347,270	$20,838,715	$21,439,365

Years to Retirement: 30

Annual Withdrawal Percentage: 4.5%

Table B: The Amount You Could Safely Withdraw from Your Savings Each Year

| Additions: Monthly | $100 | $200 | $400 | $700 | $1,000 | $1,375 | $1,833 |
Yearly	$1,200	$2,400	$4,800	$8,400	$12,000	$16,500	$22,000
Current Balance							
$ -	$5,897	$11,795	$23,589	$41,281	$58,973	$81,088	$108,118
$ 10,000	$10,181	$16,078	$27,873	$45,565	$63,257	$85,372	$112,401
$ 20,000	$14,464	$20,361	$32,156	$49,848	$67,540	$89,655	$116,684
$ 30,000	$18,747	$24,644	$36,439	$54,131	$71,823	$93,938	$120,967
$ 40,000	$23,030	$28,928	$40,722	$58,414	$76,106	$98,221	$125,251
$ 50,000	$27,314	$33,211	$45,006	$62,698	$80,390	$102,505	$129,534
$ 60,000	$31,597	$37,494	$49,289	$66,981	$84,673	$106,788	$133,817
$ 70,000	$35,880	$41,778	$53,572	$71,264	$88,956	$111,071	$138,101
$ 80,000	$40,163	$46,061	$57,855	$75,548	$93,240	$115,355	$142,384
$ 90,000	$44,447	$50,344	$62,139	$79,831	$97,523	$119,638	$146,667
$ 100,000	$48,730	$54,627	$66,422	$84,114	$101,806	$123,921	$150,950
$ 125,000	$59,438	$65,336	$77,130	$94,822	$112,514	$134,629	$161,659
$ 150,000	$70,146	$76,044	$87,838	$105,530	$123,222	$145,337	$172,367
$ 175,000	$80,855	$86,752	$98,547	$116,239	$133,931	$156,046	$183,075
$ 200,000	$91,563	$97,460	$109,255	$126,947	$144,639	$166,754	$193,783
$ 225,000	$102,271	$108,168	$119,963	$137,655	$155,347	$177,462	$204,491
$ 250,000	$112,979	$118,876	$130,671	$148,363	$166,055	$188,170	$215,199
$ 300,000	$134,395	$140,293	$152,087	$169,779	$187,471	$209,586	$236,616
$ 350,000	$155,812	$161,709	$173,504	$191,196	$208,888	$231,003	$258,032
$ 400,000	$177,228	$183,125	$194,920	$212,612	$230,304	$252,419	$279,448
$ 500,000	$220,061	$225,958	$237,753	$255,445	$273,137	$295,252	$322,281
$ 750,000	$327,143	$333,040	$344,835	$362,527	$380,219	$402,334	$429,363
$1,000,000	$434,224	$440,122	$451,916	$469,608	$487,300	$509,415	$536,445
$2,000,000	$862,551	$868,448	$880,243	$897,935	$915,627	$937,742	$964,771

Years to Retirement: 35

Annualized Return Guesstimate: 8.0%

Table A: The Future Value of Your Savings

Additions: Monthly	$100	$200	$400	$700	$1,000	$1,375	$1,833
Yearly	$1,200	$2,400	$4,800	$8,400	$12,000	$16,500	$22,000
Current Balance							
$ -	$206,780	$413,560	$827,121	$1,447,461	$2,067,802	$2,843,227	$3,790,963
$ 10,000	$354,634	$561,414	$974,974	$1,595,315	$2,215,655	$2,991,081	$3,938,816
$ 20,000	$502,487	$709,267	$1,122,828	$1,743,168	$2,363,509	$3,138,934	$4,086,670
$ 30,000	$650,340	$857,121	$1,270,681	$1,891,021	$2,511,362	$3,286,788	$4,234,523
$ 40,000	$798,194	$1,004,974	$1,418,534	$2,038,875	$2,659,215	$3,434,641	$4,382,377
$ 50,000	$946,047	$1,152,828	$1,566,388	$2,186,728	$2,807,069	$3,582,494	$4,530,230
$ 60,000	$1,093,901	$1,300,681	$1,714,241	$2,334,582	$2,954,922	$3,730,348	$4,678,083
$ 70,000	$1,241,754	$1,448,534	$1,862,095	$2,482,435	$3,102,776	$3,878,201	$4,825,937
$ 80,000	$1,389,608	$1,596,388	$2,009,948	$2,630,289	$3,250,629	$4,026,055	$4,973,790
$ 90,000	$1,537,461	$1,744,241	$2,157,802	$2,778,142	$3,398,483	$4,173,908	$5,121,644
$ 100,000	$1,685,315	$1,892,095	$2,305,655	$2,925,996	$3,546,336	$4,321,762	$5,269,497
$ 125,000	$2,054,948	$2,261,728	$2,675,289	$3,295,629	$3,915,970	$4,691,395	$5,639,131
$ 150,000	$2,424,582	$2,631,362	$3,044,922	$3,665,263	$4,285,603	$5,061,029	$6,008,764
$ 175,000	$2,794,215	$3,000,996	$3,414,556	$4,034,896	$4,655,237	$5,430,663	$6,378,398
$ 200,000	$3,163,849	$3,370,629	$3,784,190	$4,404,530	$5,024,871	$5,800,296	$6,748,032
$ 225,000	$3,533,483	$3,740,263	$4,153,823	$4,774,164	$5,394,504	$6,169,930	$7,117,665
$ 250,000	$3,903,116	$4,109,896	$4,523,457	$5,143,797	$5,764,138	$6,539,563	$7,487,299
$ 300,000	$4,642,383	$4,849,164	$5,262,724	$5,883,064	$6,503,405	$7,278,831	$8,226,566
$ 350,000	$5,381,651	$5,588,431	$6,001,991	$6,622,332	$7,242,672	$8,018,098	$8,965,833
$ 400,000	$6,120,918	$6,327,698	$6,741,258	$7,361,599	$7,981,939	$8,757,365	$9,705,101
$ 500,000	$7,599,452	$7,806,232	$8,219,793	$8,840,133	$9,460,474	$10,235,899	$11,183,635
$ 750,000	$11,295,788	$11,502,569	$11,916,129	$12,536,469	$13,156,810	$13,932,235	$14,879,971
$ 1,000,000	$14,992,124	$15,198,905	$15,612,465	$16,232,805	$16,853,146	$17,628,572	$18,576,307
$ 2,000,000	$29,777,469	$29,984,249	$30,397,809	$31,018,150	$31,638,490	$32,413,916	$33,361,651

Years to Retirement: 35

Annual Withdrawal Percentage: 4.5%

Table B: The Amount You Could Safely Withdraw from Your Savings Each Year

Additions: Monthly / Yearly	$100 / $1,200	$200 / $2,400	$400 / $4,800	$700 / $8,400	$1,000 / $12,000	$1,375 / $16,500	$1,833 / $22,000
Current Balance							
$ -	$9,305	$18,610	$37,220	$65,136	$93,051	$127,945	$170,593
$ 10,000	$15,959	$25,264	$43,874	$71,789	$99,704	$134,599	$177,247
$ 20,000	$22,612	$31,917	$50,527	$78,443	$106,358	$141,252	$183,900
$ 30,000	$29,265	$38,570	$57,181	$85,096	$113,011	$147,905	$190,554
$ 40,000	$35,919	$45,224	$63,834	$91,749	$119,665	$154,559	$197,207
$ 50,000	$42,572	$51,877	$70,487	$98,403	$126,318	$161,212	$203,860
$ 60,000	$49,226	$58,531	$77,141	$105,056	$132,972	$167,866	$210,514
$ 70,000	$55,879	$65,184	$83,794	$111,710	$139,625	$174,519	$217,167
$ 80,000	$62,532	$71,837	$90,448	$118,363	$146,278	$181,172	$223,821
$ 90,000	$69,186	$78,491	$97,101	$125,016	$152,932	$187,826	$230,474
$ 100,000	$75,839	$85,144	$103,754	$131,670	$159,585	$194,479	$237,127
$ 125,000	$92,473	$101,778	$120,388	$148,303	$176,219	$211,113	$253,761
$ 150,000	$109,106	$118,411	$137,022	$164,937	$192,852	$227,746	$270,394
$ 175,000	$125,740	$135,045	$153,655	$181,570	$209,486	$244,380	$287,028
$ 200,000	$142,373	$151,678	$170,289	$198,204	$226,119	$261,013	$303,661
$ 225,000	$159,007	$168,312	$186,922	$214,837	$242,753	$277,647	$320,295
$ 250,000	$175,640	$184,945	$203,556	$231,471	$259,386	$294,280	$336,928
$ 300,000	$208,907	$218,212	$236,823	$264,738	$292,653	$327,547	$370,195
$ 350,000	$242,174	$251,479	$270,090	$298,005	$325,920	$360,814	$403,462
$ 400,000	$275,441	$284,746	$303,357	$331,272	$359,187	$394,081	$436,730
$ 500,000	$341,975	$351,280	$369,891	$397,806	$425,721	$460,615	$503,264
$ 750,000	$508,310	$517,616	$536,226	$564,141	$592,056	$626,951	$669,599
$ 1,000,000	$674,646	$683,951	$702,561	$730,476	$758,392	$793,286	$835,934
$ 2,000,000	$1,339,986	$1,349,291	$1,367,901	$1,395,817	$1,423,732	$1,458,626	$1,501,274

95

Annualized Return Guesstimate: 8.2%

Table A: The Future Value of Your Savings

Additions: Monthly	$100	$200	$400	$700	$1,000	$1,375	$1,833
Yearly	$1,200	$2,400	$4,800	$8,400	$12,000	$16,500	$22,000
Current Balance							
$ -	$327,706	$655,412	$1,310,824	$2,293,942	$3,277,060	$4,505,957	$6,007,932
$ 10,000	$561,638	$889,344	$1,544,756	$2,527,874	$3,510,992	$4,739,890	$6,241,865
$ 20,000	$795,571	$1,123,277	$1,778,689	$2,761,807	$3,744,925	$4,973,822	$6,475,797
$ 30,000	$1,029,503	$1,357,209	$2,012,621	$2,995,739	$3,978,857	$5,207,755	$6,709,730
$ 40,000	$1,263,436	$1,591,142	$2,246,554	$3,229,672	$4,212,790	$5,441,687	$6,943,662
$ 50,000	$1,497,368	$1,825,074	$2,480,486	$3,463,604	$4,446,722	$5,675,620	$7,177,594
$ 60,000	$1,731,301	$2,059,007	$2,714,419	$3,697,537	$4,680,655	$5,909,552	$7,411,527
$ 70,000	$1,965,233	$2,292,939	$2,948,351	$3,931,469	$4,914,587	$6,143,484	$7,645,459
$ 80,000	$2,199,165	$2,526,871	$3,182,283	$4,165,401	$5,148,519	$6,377,417	$7,879,392
$ 90,000	$2,433,098	$2,760,804	$3,416,216	$4,399,334	$5,382,452	$6,611,349	$8,113,324
$ 100,000	$2,667,030	$2,994,736	$3,650,148	$4,633,266	$5,616,384	$6,845,282	$8,347,257
$ 125,000	$3,251,861	$3,579,567	$4,234,979	$5,218,097	$6,201,215	$7,430,113	$8,932,088
$ 150,000	$3,836,692	$4,164,398	$4,819,810	$5,802,928	$6,786,046	$8,014,944	$9,516,919
$ 175,000	$4,421,524	$4,749,230	$5,404,641	$6,387,759	$7,370,877	$8,599,775	$10,101,750
$ 200,000	$5,006,355	$5,334,061	$5,989,473	$6,972,591	$7,955,709	$9,184,606	$10,686,581
$ 225,000	$5,591,186	$5,918,892	$6,574,304	$7,557,422	$8,540,540	$9,769,437	$11,271,412
$ 250,000	$6,176,017	$6,503,723	$7,159,135	$8,142,253	$9,125,371	$10,354,268	$11,856,243
$ 300,000	$7,345,679	$7,673,385	$8,328,797	$9,311,915	$10,295,033	$11,523,930	$13,026,905
$ 350,000	$8,515,341	$8,843,047	$9,498,459	$10,481,577	$11,464,695	$12,693,592	$14,195,567
$ 400,000	$9,685,003	$10,012,709	$10,668,121	$11,651,239	$12,634,357	$13,863,255	$15,365,229
$ 500,000	$12,024,327	$12,352,033	$13,007,445	$13,990,563	$14,973,681	$16,202,579	$17,704,554
$ 750,000	$17,872,638	$18,200,344	$18,855,756	$19,838,874	$20,821,992	$22,050,890	$23,552,864
$ 1,000,000	$23,720,949	$24,048,656	$24,704,067	$25,687,185	$26,670,303	$27,899,200	$29,401,175
$ 2,000,000	$47,114,192	$47,441,898	$48,097,310	$49,080,428	$50,063,546	$51,292,443	$52,794,418

Years to Retirement: 40

Annual Withdrawal Percentage: 4.5%

Table B: The Amount You Could Safely Withdraw from Your Savings Each Year

| Additions: Monthly | $100 | $200 | $400 | $700 | $1,000 | $1,375 | $1,833 |
Yearly	$1,200	$2,400	$4,800	$8,400	$12,000	$16,500	$22,000
Current Balance							
$ -	$14,747	$29,494	$58,987	$103,227	$147,468	$202,768	$270,357
$ 10,000	$25,274	$40,020	$69,514	$113,754	$157,995	$213,295	$280,884
$ 20,000	$35,801	$50,547	$80,041	$124,281	$168,522	$223,822	$291,411
$ 30,000	$46,328	$61,074	$90,568	$134,808	$179,049	$234,349	$301,938
$ 40,000	$56,855	$71,601	$101,095	$145,335	$189,576	$244,876	$312,465
$ 50,000	$67,382	$82,128	$111,622	$155,862	$200,102	$255,403	$322,992
$ 60,000	$77,909	$92,655	$122,149	$166,389	$210,629	$265,930	$333,519
$ 70,000	$88,435	$103,182	$132,676	$176,916	$221,156	$276,457	$344,046
$ 80,000	$98,962	$113,709	$143,203	$187,443	$231,683	$286,984	$354,573
$ 90,000	$109,489	$124,236	$153,730	$197,970	$242,210	$297,511	$365,100
$ 100,000	$120,016	$134,763	$164,257	$208,497	$252,737	$308,038	$375,627
$ 125,000	$146,334	$161,081	$190,574	$234,814	$279,055	$334,355	$401,944
$ 150,000	$172,651	$187,398	$216,891	$261,132	$305,372	$360,672	$428,261
$ 175,000	$198,969	$213,715	$243,209	$287,449	$331,689	$386,990	$454,579
$ 200,000	$225,286	$240,033	$269,526	$313,767	$358,007	$413,307	$480,896
$ 225,000	$251,603	$266,350	$295,844	$340,084	$384,324	$439,625	$507,214
$ 250,000	$277,921	$292,668	$322,161	$366,401	$410,642	$465,942	$533,531
$ 300,000	$330,556	$345,302	$374,796	$419,036	$463,276	$518,577	$586,166
$ 350,000	$383,190	$397,937	$427,431	$471,671	$515,911	$571,212	$638,801
$ 400,000	$435,825	$450,572	$480,065	$524,306	$568,546	$623,846	$691,435
$ 500,000	$541,095	$555,842	$585,335	$629,575	$673,816	$729,116	$796,705
$ 750,000	$804,269	$819,015	$848,509	$892,749	$936,990	$992,290	$1,059,879
$1,000,000	$1,067,443	$1,082,189	$1,111,683	$1,155,923	$1,200,164	$1,255,464	$1,323,053
$2,000,000	$2,120,139	$2,134,885	$2,164,379	$2,208,619	$2,252,860	$2,308,160	$2,375,749

Years to Retirement: 45

Annualized Return Guesstimate: 8.4%

Table A: The Future Value of Your Savings

| Additions: Monthly | $100 | $200 | $400 | $700 | $1,000 | $1,375 | $1,833 |
Yearly	$1,200	$2,400	$4,800	$8,400	$12,000	$16,500	$22,000
Current Balance							
$ -	$524,256	$1,048,513	$2,097,026	$3,669,795	$5,242,564	$7,208,525	$9,611,350
$ 10,000	$901,236	$1,425,492	$2,474,005	$4,046,774	$5,619,543	$7,585,505	$9,988,329
$ 20,000	$1,278,215	$1,802,472	$2,850,984	$4,423,754	$5,996,523	$7,962,484	$10,365,309
$ 30,000	$1,655,195	$2,179,451	$3,227,964	$4,800,733	$6,373,502	$8,339,464	$10,742,288
$ 40,000	$2,032,174	$2,556,431	$3,604,943	$5,177,713	$6,750,482	$8,716,443	$11,119,267
$ 50,000	$2,409,154	$2,933,410	$3,981,923	$5,554,692	$7,127,461	$9,093,423	$11,496,247
$ 60,000	$2,786,133	$3,310,390	$4,358,902	$5,931,672	$7,504,441	$9,470,402	$11,873,226
$ 70,000	$3,163,113	$3,687,369	$4,735,882	$6,308,651	$7,881,420	$9,847,382	$12,250,206
$ 80,000	$3,540,092	$4,064,349	$5,112,861	$6,685,630	$8,258,400	$10,224,361	$12,627,185
$ 90,000	$3,917,072	$4,441,328	$5,489,841	$7,062,610	$8,635,379	$10,601,341	$13,004,165
$ 100,000	$4,294,051	$4,818,307	$5,866,820	$7,439,589	$9,012,359	$10,978,320	$13,381,144
$ 125,000	$5,236,500	$5,760,756	$6,809,269	$8,382,038	$9,954,807	$11,920,769	$14,323,593
$ 150,000	$6,178,948	$6,703,205	$7,751,718	$9,324,487	$10,897,256	$12,863,217	$15,266,042
$ 175,000	$7,121,397	$7,645,653	$8,694,166	$10,266,935	$11,839,705	$13,805,666	$16,208,490
$ 200,000	$8,063,846	$8,588,102	$9,636,615	$11,209,384	$12,782,153	$14,748,115	$17,150,939
$ 225,000	$9,006,294	$9,530,551	$10,579,064	$12,151,833	$13,724,602	$15,690,563	$18,093,388
$ 250,000	$9,948,743	$10,473,000	$11,521,512	$13,094,281	$14,667,051	$16,633,012	$19,035,836
$ 300,000	$11,833,640	$12,357,897	$13,406,410	$14,979,179	$16,551,948	$18,517,909	$20,920,734
$ 350,000	$13,718,538	$14,242,794	$15,291,307	$16,864,076	$18,436,845	$20,402,807	$22,805,631
$ 400,000	$15,603,435	$16,127,692	$17,176,204	$18,748,973	$20,321,743	$22,287,704	$24,690,528
$ 500,000	$19,373,230	$19,897,486	$20,945,999	$22,518,768	$24,091,537	$26,057,499	$28,460,323
$ 750,000	$28,797,717	$29,321,973	$30,370,486	$31,943,255	$33,516,024	$35,481,986	$37,884,810
$ 1,000,000	$38,222,203	$38,746,460	$39,794,973	$41,367,742	$42,940,511	$44,906,472	$47,309,297
$ 2,000,000	$75,920,150	$76,444,407	$77,492,919	$79,065,689	$80,638,458	$82,604,419	$85,007,244

Years to Retirement: 45   Annual Withdrawal Percentage: 4.5%

Table B: The Amount You Could Safely Withdraw from Your Savings Each Year

| Additions: Monthly | $100 | $200 | $400 | $700 | $1,000 | $1,375 | $1,833 |
Yearly	$1,200	$2,400	$4,800	$8,400	$12,000	$16,500	$22,000
Current Balance							
$ -	$23,592	$47,183	$94,366	$165,141	$235,915	$324,384	$432,511
$ 10,000	$40,556	$64,147	$111,330	$182,105	$252,879	$341,348	$449,475
$ 20,000	$57,520	$81,111	$128,294	$199,069	$269,844	$358,312	$466,439
$ 30,000	$74,484	$98,075	$145,258	$216,033	$286,808	$375,276	$483,403
$ 40,000	$91,448	$115,039	$162,222	$232,997	$303,772	$392,240	$500,367
$ 50,000	$108,412	$132,003	$179,187	$249,961	$320,736	$409,204	$517,331
$ 60,000	$125,376	$148,968	$196,151	$266,925	$337,700	$426,168	$534,295
$ 70,000	$142,340	$165,932	$213,115	$283,889	$354,664	$443,132	$551,259
$ 80,000	$159,304	$182,896	$230,079	$300,853	$371,628	$460,096	$568,223
$ 90,000	$176,268	$199,860	$247,043	$317,817	$388,592	$477,060	$585,187
$ 100,000	$193,232	$216,824	$264,007	$334,782	$405,556	$494,024	$602,151
$ 125,000	$235,642	$259,234	$306,417	$377,192	$447,966	$536,435	$644,562
$ 150,000	$278,053	$301,644	$348,827	$419,602	$490,377	$578,845	$686,972
$ 175,000	$320,463	$344,054	$391,237	$462,012	$532,787	$621,255	$729,382
$ 200,000	$362,873	$386,465	$433,648	$504,422	$575,197	$663,665	$771,792
$ 225,000	$405,283	$428,875	$476,058	$546,832	$617,607	$706,075	$814,202
$ 250,000	$447,693	$471,285	$518,468	$589,243	$660,017	$748,486	$856,613
$ 300,000	$532,514	$556,105	$603,288	$674,063	$744,838	$833,306	$941,433
$ 350,000	$617,334	$640,926	$688,109	$758,883	$829,658	$918,126	$1,026,253
$ 400,000	$702,155	$725,746	$772,929	$843,704	$914,478	$1,002,947	$1,111,074
$ 500,000	$871,795	$895,387	$942,570	$1,013,345	$1,084,119	$1,172,587	$1,280,715
$ 750,000	$1,295,897	$1,319,489	$1,366,672	$1,437,446	$1,508,221	$1,596,689	$1,704,816
$ 1,000,000	$1,719,999	$1,743,591	$1,790,774	$1,861,548	$1,932,323	$2,020,791	$2,128,918
$ 2,000,000	$3,416,407	$3,439,998	$3,487,181	$3,557,956	$3,628,731	$3,717,199	$3,825,326

Annualized Return Guesstimate: 8.6%

Table A: The Future Value of Your Savings

Additions: Monthly / Yearly	$100 / $1,200	$200 / $2,400	$400 / $4,800	$700 / $8,400	$1,000 / $12,000	$1,375 / $16,500	$1,833 / $22,000
Current Balance							
$ -	$849,371	$1,698,742	$3,397,484	$5,945,597	$8,493,710	$11,678,851	$15,571,773
$ 10,000	$1,468,087	$2,317,458	$4,016,200	$6,564,313	$9,112,426	$12,297,567	$16,190,489
$ 20,000	$2,086,803	$2,936,174	$4,634,916	$7,183,029	$9,731,142	$12,916,283	$16,809,205
$ 30,000	$2,705,519	$3,554,890	$5,253,632	$7,801,745	$10,349,858	$13,534,999	$17,427,921
$ 40,000	$3,324,235	$4,173,606	$5,872,347	$8,420,460	$10,968,573	$14,153,715	$18,046,637
$ 50,000	$3,942,950	$4,792,321	$6,491,063	$9,039,176	$11,587,289	$14,772,431	$18,665,353
$ 60,000	$4,561,666	$5,411,037	$7,109,779	$9,657,892	$12,206,005	$15,391,146	$19,284,069
$ 70,000	$5,180,382	$6,029,753	$7,728,495	$10,276,608	$12,824,721	$16,009,862	$19,902,784
$ 80,000	$5,799,098	$6,648,469	$8,347,211	$10,895,324	$13,443,437	$16,628,578	$20,521,500
$ 90,000	$6,417,814	$7,267,185	$8,965,927	$11,514,040	$14,062,153	$17,247,294	$21,140,216
$ 100,000	$7,036,530	$7,885,901	$9,584,643	$12,132,756	$14,680,869	$17,866,010	$21,758,932
$ 125,000	$8,583,319	$9,432,690	$11,131,432	$13,679,545	$16,227,658	$19,412,800	$23,305,722
$ 150,000	$10,130,109	$10,979,480	$12,678,222	$15,226,335	$17,774,448	$20,959,589	$24,852,511
$ 175,000	$11,676,899	$12,526,270	$14,225,012	$16,773,125	$19,321,238	$22,506,379	$26,399,301
$ 200,000	$13,223,689	$14,073,060	$15,771,802	$18,319,915	$20,868,028	$24,053,169	$27,946,091
$ 225,000	$14,770,478	$15,619,849	$17,318,591	$19,866,704	$22,414,817	$25,599,958	$29,492,881
$ 250,000	$16,317,268	$17,166,639	$18,865,381	$21,413,494	$23,961,607	$27,146,748	$31,039,670
$ 300,000	$19,410,847	$20,260,218	$21,958,960	$24,507,073	$27,055,186	$30,240,328	$34,133,250
$ 350,000	$22,504,427	$23,353,798	$25,052,540	$27,600,653	$30,148,766	$33,333,907	$37,226,829
$ 400,000	$25,598,006	$26,447,377	$28,146,119	$30,694,232	$33,242,345	$36,427,486	$40,320,408
$ 500,000	$31,785,165	$32,634,536	$34,333,278	$36,881,391	$39,429,504	$42,614,645	$46,507,567
$ 750,000	$47,253,062	$48,102,433	$49,801,175	$52,349,288	$54,897,401	$58,082,542	$61,975,464
$1,000,000	$62,720,959	$63,570,330	$65,269,072	$67,817,185	$70,365,298	$73,550,439	$77,443,361

Years to Retirement: 50

Annual Withdrawal Percentage: 4.5%

Table B: The Amount You Could Safely Withdraw from Your Savings Each Year

Additions: Monthly	$100	$200	$400	$700	$1,000	$1,375	$1,833
Yearly	$1,200	$2,400	$4,800	$8,400	$12,000	$16,500	$22,000
Current Balance							
$ -	$38,222	$76,443	$152,887	$267,552	$382,217	$525,548	$700,730
$ 10,000	$66,064	$104,286	$180,729	$295,394	$410,059	$553,391	$728,572
$ 20,000	$93,906	$132,128	$208,571	$323,236	$437,901	$581,233	$756,414
$ 30,000	$121,748	$159,970	$236,413	$351,079	$465,744	$609,075	$784,256
$ 40,000	$149,591	$187,812	$264,256	$378,921	$493,586	$636,917	$812,099
$ 50,000	$177,433	$215,654	$292,098	$406,763	$521,428	$664,759	$839,941
$ 60,000	$205,275	$243,497	$319,940	$434,605	$549,270	$692,602	$867,783
$ 70,000	$233,117	$271,339	$347,782	$462,447	$577,112	$720,444	$895,625
$ 80,000	$260,959	$299,181	$375,624	$490,290	$604,955	$748,286	$923,468
$ 90,000	$288,802	$327,023	$403,467	$518,132	$632,797	$776,128	$951,310
$ 100,000	$316,644	$354,866	$431,309	$545,974	$660,639	$803,970	$979,152
$ 125,000	$386,249	$424,471	$500,914	$615,580	$730,245	$873,576	$1,048,757
$ 150,000	$455,855	$494,077	$570,520	$685,185	$799,850	$943,182	$1,118,363
$ 175,000	$525,460	$563,682	$640,126	$754,791	$869,456	$1,012,787	$1,187,969
$ 200,000	$595,066	$633,288	$709,731	$824,396	$939,061	$1,082,393	$1,257,574
$ 225,000	$664,672	$702,893	$779,337	$894,002	$1,008,667	$1,151,998	$1,327,180
$ 250,000	$734,277	$772,499	$848,942	$963,607	$1,078,272	$1,221,604	$1,396,785
$ 300,000	$873,488	$911,710	$988,153	$1,102,818	$1,217,483	$1,360,815	$1,535,996
$ 350,000	$1,012,699	$1,050,921	$1,127,364	$1,242,029	$1,356,694	$1,500,026	$1,675,207
$ 400,000	$1,151,910	$1,190,132	$1,266,575	$1,381,240	$1,495,906	$1,639,237	$1,814,418
$ 500,000	$1,430,332	$1,468,554	$1,544,998	$1,659,663	$1,774,328	$1,917,659	$2,092,841
$ 750,000	$2,126,388	$2,164,609	$2,241,053	$2,355,718	$2,470,383	$2,613,714	$2,788,896
$ 1,000,000	$2,822,443	$2,860,665	$2,937,108	$3,051,773	$3,166,438	$3,309,770	$3,484,951

About the Author

Ron Elmer, MBA, CFA, CPA, CFP®, is Chief Investment Strategist of Realm Investment Consulting, an independent investment research and consulting firm. Previously, Ron was the director of equity research at NCM Capital, where he managed a team of investment professionals and large cap and mid cap portfolios for institutional clients such as IBM, Walgreens, Boeing, the State of Georgia, and the California State Teachers Retirement System. Formerly Ron was the head of equities for the investment management division of First Citizens Bank (North Carolina), where he managed over $2 billion of active- and passive-indexed equity portfolios for many clients, including the State of North Carolina Retirement System and Campbell University. Prior to that, he worked as an investment analyst for a $2 billion pension fund at Warner-Lambert Company (now Pfizer).

Ron earned a BBA in finance from the University of Oklahoma and an MBA in finance and accounting from New York University. He once held the Education Chair as a member of the board of directors of the North Carolina Society of Financial Analysts, and he has taught finance courses at Strayer University and North Carolina State University. Ron has earned the CFA (Chartered Financial Analyst) and CFP® (Certified Financial Planner™) designations and holds CPA (Certified Public Accountant) certificates in the states of Maryland and North Carolina.

Ron grew up in Great Falls, Montana where he graduated from C.M. Russell High School. He now lives near Raleigh, North Carolina with his wife and 6-year old boy/girl twins.

Notes:

Certified Financial Planner Board of Standards, Inc. owns the certification marks CFP®, Certified Financial Planner™, and CFP (with flame logo)® in the United States, which it awards to individuals who successfully complete CFP Board's initial and ongoing certification requirements, including continuing education requirements. CFP® certification is granted solely by Certified Financial Planner Board of Standards, Inc. to individuals who, in addition to completing an educational requirement such as this CFP Board-Registered Program, have met ethics, experience, and examination requirements.

The Chartered Financial Analyst, or CFA, designation is granted solely by the CFA Institute to individuals who, in addition to completing certain educational requirements, have met ethics and experience requirements and passed three rigorous examinations.

CPSIA information can be obtained at www.ICGtesting.com
Printed in the USA
LVOW090528040413

327567LV00001B/8/P